ROYAL ALBUM

THE QUEEN at 90

WHY THE QUEEN MATTERS

THE QUEEN AT 90

It's a remarkable age for anyone to live to, but for Her Majesty Queen Elizabeth II it is especially significant. She becomes the first British monarch to have lived to 90. Queen Victoria was previously the oldest-lived female monarch and died at age 81. On the male side, King George III lived to 81 as well.

And Queen Elizabeth II has done this while living her entire life in the public eye. Monarchs have always been at the centre of the nation but as the 20th century progressed, and turned over into the 21st century, the spotlight on the Royal Family has grown brighter and brighter. The world's media watches her every move. There may be no more closely-watched and heavily scrutinised family in the world. Certainly not one for so long and so consistently. She has been critiqued her entire life and has still managed to maintain the same dignity and composure that we have come to know and love about her. And, importantly, she has endeavoured to pass on those qualities to other members of her family, so that her legacy will live on, even when she is gone.

And to think it all started in such relatively unremarkable fashion. Her birth got some attention, after all she was the eldest daughter of the second-in-line to the throne, but she was hardly expected to play a great role in British history given her father was not King. It was a fateful decision by her uncle in 1936 to abdicate and pass the crown onto her father that guaranteed young Princess Elizabeth's life would never be the same again. All of a sudden she became the heir-apparent. And then, when her own father passed away, she became Queen.

The world is very different from the one that saw a young woman have a crown placed on her head at Westminster Abbey on 6 February 1952. The grainy black and white television images of that day have now been transformed into vivid high-definition colour. The entire planet seemed to get smaller as technology and speed of travel improved beyond anyone's imagination. Governments and heads of state have come and gone, both within the United Kingdom and abroad. Nations have come into being, have ceased to exist, or have shifted borders. There have been wars, disasters and global tragedies. But there have also been moments when the world has come together. Technological and medical achievements. People on the moon. The birth of the internet. And with all of this happening around her, Queen Elizabeth II has remained a rock of consistency.

Her Majesty's 90th birthday celebrations and commemorations are as big as the United Kingdom has ever seen. It's testament to her enduring appeal over the decades. Even during the royal family's most trying times (and there have been plenty of those) her own popularity has rarely suffered.

She succeeded her father at a time when the United Kingdom's place in the world was beginning to shift. The idea that the world was shaped by the influence of the United Kingdom was well and truly in decline. For the first half of the 20th century, the United Kingdom had firmly held its place as one of the global superpowers but the Second World War began a shift towards a new world where the power and influence of the UK would recede. It's military and economic might diminished as the United States and Soviet Union took over as post-war superpowers. In spite of all that, the Queen has been able to show off the best of the United Kingdom to the rest of the world.

Like all people, Her Majesty has experienced her share of family tragedy. She has watched as the marriages of some of those closest to her have crumbled. Loved ones have died – her father, her mother, and her younger sister included. The tragic death of her eldest son's first wife, Diana, Princess of Wales rocked the royal family and shook the public's confidence in it. But through all this she has remained resolute, even under the close gaze of the press, who have been desperate for any sort of scandal they can brush the royal family with. Her priorities have always been to support her family, her nation and her Commonwealth.

Her appeal does not lie solely within the United Kingdom either. Her reign has coincided with the rise of the jet-travel era, when travelling the globe has never been easier. Over the course of 60 years she has undertaken 261 official overseas visits, including 78 state visits, to a massive 116 countries. Millions of people have waited to catch even just a glimpse of her from afar.

She has met Presidents, Prime Ministers, fellow Kings and Queens, Popes and other religious leaders. And there have been countless others, from all walks of life, who've had the honour to be introduced to the Queen. Through all this she has been a warm and welcoming woman, who has carried herself with dignity and been a superb ambassador for the United Kingdom and Commonwealth.

The Queen has represented the British monarchy so superbly that there has never been any serious thought to doing away with the system at all. Even as the rise of people-power across the globe makes institutions like the monarchy look quaint and old-fashioned, its defenders point to Her Majesty and the royal family as the ideal way for the system to continue. Though always staying informed of her governments' actions over the years, the Queen has always been at great pains to stay above the fray and remain as impartial and apolitical as ever.

The monarchy is more than just a money-spinner for British tourism. It remains because it shows the best of the United Kingdom to the world. It's dignity. It's the ability to stay stoic even in the face of great danger. It's the ability to bring the nation together during times of great sadness. And it's all because of how one woman has carried herself over 90 years.

There will come a day when Queen Elizabeth II is no longer with us. Her advancing age is a constant reminder of that sad reality. But when that time comes, there will be no harsh words. The world will recognise a remarkable woman who represented her family and her country to the absolute best of her ability.

2016 IS A YEAR TO REMEMBER

Her Majesty Queen Elizabeth II will turn 90 years old on 21 April 2016.

Born in 1926, Elizabeth's life has been nothing short of remarkable. She began as the daughter of Prince Albert and Lady Elizabeth Bowes-Lyon. She was never expected to become Queen but the abdication of her uncle King Edward VIII in 1936 changed everything. All of a sudden her father was King George VI and she was the next in the line of succession.

Royal Album – The Queen at 90 recounts this remarkable woman's fascinating life. There have been plenty of moments to be proud – her wedding, her coronation, her jubilees, as well as the birth of her children, grandchildren and great-grandchildren. She has celebrated each of these events with the people of the United Kingdom and all around the world who admire her.

But no life is free of heartache and tragedy. Her family has endured marriage breakdowns, and the deaths of loved ones. But throughout all this Queen Elizabeth II has been a pillar of strength. The United Kingdom has often looked to her to guide them through difficult times and she has never let them down.

As the Queen approaches her 90th birthday, she continues to perform her duties with the same dignity and enthusiasm she always has. In 2014 and 2015 she welcomed the leaders of Ireland and Singapore. Though her advancing age means her travel schedule has lightened considerably, she has been able to make visits to Italy, France, Northern Ireland and Germany. And she has been able to watch with pride as her family celebrates the birth of another Princess.

Her 90th birthday will be special. The United Kingdom, and the entire world, will be ready to celebrate it with her.

Britain's Queen Elizabeth (R) and Prince Philip ride in the Golden State Carriage at the head of a parade from Buckingham Palace to St Paul's Cathedral celebrating the Queen's Golden Jubilee, June 4, 2002

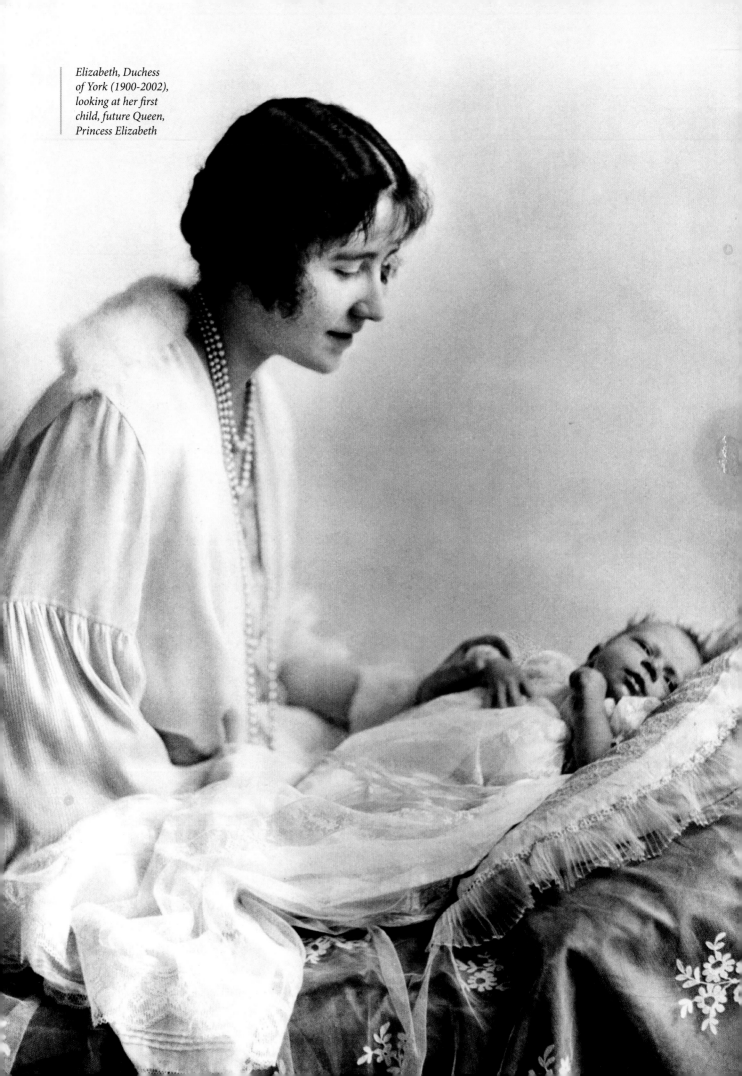

Elizabeth, Duchess of York (1900-2002), looking at her first child, future Queen, Princess Elizabeth

A FUTURE QUEEN IS BORN

In the early hours of 21 April 1926 – at approximately 2.40am – a baby girl was born in London. Little did the mother, father, doctors and anyone else present that morning know just how important this young child would be. She would grow up to become one of the most influential people of the 20th and 21st centuries.

That's not to say the birth passed by without any sort of commotion. After all this was no ordinary birth. The mother and father were no ordinary British citizens. They were royalty. This was the first child for the Duke and Duchess of York, Prince Albert and Elizabeth. Prince Albert was the second oldest son of King George V and Queen Mary, and second in the line of succession for the British throne. Until his elder brother married and had his own children, any child of Prince Albert's would go immediately after him in the line of succession. If nothing else, this birth would make the King extremely happy. He would become a grandfather to a third child.

As the Duchess went into labour, the United Kingdom was in the midst of national turmoil. A coal miner's dispute was causing all sorts of headaches for the country, and especially the Conservative government.

The general council of the Trades Union Congress wanted to force the government to act to prevent wage reduction and the worsening of conditions for some 800,000 locked out coal miners.

As these negotiations continued, in those small hours of 21 April, a sleep-deprived Home Secretary, Sir William Joyson-Hicks, received a telephone call. It instructed him to go straight to 17 Bruton Street in Mayfair.

The 25 year old Elizabeth, Duchess of York, had gone into labour some time earlier. She was now in a bedroom inside the London home of her parents, the Earl and Countess of Strathmore, two of the most prominent coal owners in the United Kingdom.

Joyson-Hicks' presence that evening was not for any subversive reason. Later inquiries would reject any popular myths about the need to 'verify' that in fact the future royal had been born. Instead, it seemed that it was merely the custom at that time that Ministers of Government be present for important occasions in the life of the royal family. Even for the birth of a child who was not expected to ascend to the throne during her life. After all she was several places down the line of succession, and as she grew she was expected to move further down.

In any case, with the Home Secretary present that morning, a girl named Elizabeth Alexandra Mary came into this world. Her names taken after her mother, and two Queens.

With the delivery assured, Joyson-Smith left the building and gave word of the child's arrival to the Lord Mayor of London. He would inform the rest of the nation that the King had another grandchild.

The Duke and Duchess of York (later King George VI and Queen Elizabeth, the Queen Mother) pictured with their daughter (later, Queen Elizabeth II) as she sleeps in a precious christening robe

It had not been an easy delivery for the Duchess. The doctors would wait until 10am to inform the public what had happened. She had so much difficulty in labour that those treating her decided that a Caesarean section should be performed. The public was unaware of this development. It was not mentioned explicitly in the doctor's statements – instead it was merely referred to as a "certain line of treatment".

In the 1920s this sort of procedure was extremely dangerous to the life of both mother and daughter. It would also lessen the likelihood of the Duchess being able to bear future children (though fortunately she did fall pregnant again and give birth to another girl).

The newspapers did take considerable interest in the news, even if the girl was not expected to become Queen.

The press still expected that the future ruler would come from the offspring of her uncle, Edward the Prince of Wales. As the King's firstborn son, he was next in line to the British throne.

At age 32, the Prince was considered to be in the prime of his life. However it was becoming a serious concern within the royal household that he had not yet found a wife. Sure there had been women in his life (some of them married, much to the King and Queen's consternation) but to that point there had been no-one the Prince of Wales had been willing to settle down with and make his wife, let alone have a child with.

So with no immediate prospect of Edward siring a heir who would be universally accepted as a future King or Queen, the newspapers decided Elizabeth was news enough, and lavished a great deal of attention on the news of her birth. There was always the slight possibility that she may one day end up Queen anyway.

A movie newsreel of that era captured several black and white images of the Duchess and Elizabeth. Under the title Britain's Baby Princess, the images offered the world their first chance to see the new baby girl. They were simple photos, showing the mother holding her daughter in her arms. A caption in the minute-long film would prove to be extremely prescient – 'She may one day be the Queen of England'.

As word of the royal birth spread throughout London, crowds gathered outside the Bruton Street home. They cheered and yelled out well-wishes to the Duke, Duchess and newborn girl. Many hoped to catch a glimpse of one of them, perhaps coming outside to acknowledge their presence or receive the many telegrams and presents that had flooded in.

They didn't spot the mother, father or little girl, but they were satisfied when they saw the King and Queen. King George V, now 58 years old, had arrived to see his third grandchild. His youngest daughter, Mary, Princess Royal, had already given birth to two grandsons.

In her diary, Queen Mary would recall her thoughts upon meeting her granddaughter for the first time. She noted the baby's 'lovely complexion and pretty fair hair'. She concluded that she was a 'little darling'.

Meanwhile, the new father couldn't contain his joy. In a letter to his mother, Prince Albert conceded that while he knew that Kings 'prefer male descendants', he hoped that the arrival of this baby would delight both grandparents. He added that he knew that his wife had always wanted a daughter.

The crowds would not leave for weeks. The mood across the United Kingdom was gloomy, and the royal birth offered a welcome distraction.

By 1 May, a general strike had been called, with some 1.7 million people walking off the job, many in transport and heavy industry. The nation was in crisis, and perhaps as a result of that many people wanted to be reminded of some good news. Even on 17 May, almost a month after the birth, the Countess of Airlie noted the throng outside the house remained so large, that the baby girl had be taken outside for her morning airing via a back entrance.

The Princess would later be officially christened Elizabeth Alexandra Mary. The ceremony took place in a private chapel at Buckingham Palace. The name Elizabeth came from her mother; the name Alexandra came from her paternal great-grandmother Queen Alexandra; and the name Mary came from her paternal grandmother Queen Mary.

In the following years, every movement of this young royal would be watched closely, not just in the United Kingdom but internationally. The world would first get to know her as Princess Elizabeth, the daughter of Prince Albert, the Duke of York. Then, interest in this young girl snowballed upon the abdication of her uncle King Edward VIII. All of a sudden she became Princess Elizabeth, daughter of King George VI, and next in line for the British throne. And finally, upon the tragic passing of her father, and for many decades thereafter, the world would get to know her as Queen Elizabeth II.

Main pic: Princess Elizabeth (later Queen Elizabeth II), daughter of Their Royal Highnesses Duke and Duchess of York

Inset left: British Royalty, The christening of Princess Elizabeth Alexandra Mary, 1926

Inset top right: British Royalty, H,M,Queen Mary of Great Britain with her grand-daughter H,R,H,Princess Elizabeth after the baby had been christened, 1926

Inset bottom right: British Royalty, H,R,H,The Duchess of York with her baby daughter Princess Elizabeth (Queen Elizabeth II), 1926

THE LITTLE PRINCESS AS A CHILD

Princess Elizabeth spent her earliest years living at 145 Piccadilly. Her parents took possession of this London townhouse shortly after her birth. It was a white terraced building, mostly indistinguishable from any of the other buildings on either side.

Elizabeth lived at the top of the house, in a suite of rooms consisting of a day nursery, a night nursery and a bathroom, all linked by a landing. There were wide windows looking down on the park outside, and it wasn't out of the ordinary for her nanny to put her in a pram and take her on a stroll through Mayfair into Hyde Park.

The building's interior design allowed Elizabeth to display some young mischief. She was fond of a game where she would fetch a small toy, like a teddy bear or ball, and drop it from the nursery level, down the stairwell, onto visitors as they arrived at the house.

Unfortunately, 145 Piccadilly is not still standing today. It did not survive the Second World War bombings of London. However the site would later be transformed into The Intercontinental Hotel Park Lane, which opened in 1975 and still operates today.

Elizabeth also spent time living at White Lodge at Richmond Park. This property belonged to the Teck family, of which Queen Mary (Elizabeth's grandmother) belonged. Today, the Royal Ballet School operates the building. Its ballet museum also contains artefacts and memorabilia from its time as a royal household.

There were also frequent trips to the countryside, to visit the homes of grandparents King George V and Queen Mary, as well as her mother's parents, the Earl and Countess of Strathmore.

As she grew into a playful and precocious young child, the Princess would receive an affectionate nickname she would carry into her older years – "Lilibet". But only those closest to her would ever be allowed to call her that.

At three years of age she made her first magazine front cover with *Time* running a special. It was certainly a big deal but little did anyone know that this was just the first front cover of many.

On 21 August 1930, at the age of four, Elizabeth gained a younger sister. Princess Margaret Rose was born. Her mother was more keen on the name Ann Margaret, explaining to Queen Mary in a letter, "I am very anxious to call her Ann Margaret, as I think Ann of York sounds pretty, and Elizabeth and Ann go so well together." Unfortunately for the Duchess, King George V was not so enthusiastic for the name, and instead gave his approval for Margaret Rose.

At six years of age, Princess Elizabeth's parents took over Royal Lodge in Windsor Great Park as their very own country home. It was here on these grounds that the Princess had her own small house, called Y Bwthyn Bach (the Little College). The people of Wales presented this to her in 1932.

Princess Elizabeth in the grounds of her London home, 145 Piccadilly with a pet dog

Princess Elizabeth of York with her grandparents, King George V and Queen Mary leaving a church service at Crathie in Aberdeenshire, Scotland, 1932

Her relationship with her grandfather was an especially loving one. King George V adored Elizabeth, and the same was especially true in reverse. When struck down by serious illness in 1929, many in the royal household couldn't help but notice that it was Princess Elizabeth's visits that lifted his spirits the most.

In 1936, her grandfather died. A sad event in anyone's life, but for this young girl it would put forward a chain of events that rocked the United Kingdom and put her life on a completely different path. At age 10, her life was about to be transformed forever.

A constitutional crisis had rocked the royal family. The Prince of Wales had succeeded his father in the normal fashion and had taken the name Edward VIII. His coronation was expected to be held the following year as it was considered inappropriate to stage such a lavish event so soon after the previous King's death.

There was just one issue. After years of bachelorhood, King Edward VIII had finally settled on a woman he wished to marry – Wallis Simpson, an American socialite.

That Ms Simpson was an American was no doubt distasteful enough for members of the British establishment so used to their royals marrying within (or at the very least within the boundaries of European royalty). But the fact that Ms Simpson was divorced, twice, made her particularly unacceptable as a suitor. Not in 1930s Britain, and certainly not for a King who was also the nominal head of the Church of England.

Ms Simpson was not new to the royal household. She had met Prince Edward in 1931, actually through another woman – Thelma, Lady Furness – who was at the time his mistress. It took until 1934 before Ms Simpson would become the Prince's new mistress, and he took an immense liking to her. He found her dominant personality appealing.

His father and mother were less than thrilled with this development. King George V was especially appalled when the Prince formally introduced Ms Simpson to his mother the Queen at Buckingham Palace that year. Normally divorcees were excluded from court.

Her critics simply couldn't accept that Ms Simpson genuinely loved the King. They instead looked at her as someone driven more by the love of money or the status that would come with becoming a royal consort.

Despite all the opposition, Edward was not to be deterred. He was in love. After his father's death, the new King made it clear he intended to marry Ms Simpson.

However the UK Government remained unmoved in its opposition. The Prime Minister, Stanley Bruce, made it clear his ministers were prepared to resign en masse should the King follow through on his plans. The King faced an ultimatum. If he wished to remain King he needed to lose Ms Simpson. If he wished to marry Ms Simpson, he would have to abdicate.

Plans were made for every possible contingency, including one where the King refused to abdicate and insisted on marrying Ms Simpson. There was an idea to perhaps conduct a civil marriage service.

But the new King eventually conceded that scenario would be extremely hard to fulfil. There was just too much opposition. So, faced with a choice between his future as a King and a future with Wallis Simpson, Edward VIII chose the latter.

On 10 December 1936, he signed his written abdication notices. His witnesses were his brothers, Prince Henry, Prince George and Prince Albert. For the latter, it was an especially trying ordeal. As the oldest brother and first in line to the throne, his brother's decision to abdicate meant he all of a sudden became the new King. He took the name George VI.

All these developments brought an end to the relatively quiet upbringing that Princess Elizabeth had previously enjoyed. While her grandfather and uncle were King, it was never widely expected that she would one day become Queen. Though kept under close watch, she was allowed a relatively free reign in childhood.

Now that her father had ascended to become King, his offspring were next in the line of succession. There was also no possibility of any more children, let alone males who would leapfrog his older sisters up the order. Elizabeth as the eldest of the two daughters was now next in line.

Below left: Princess Elizabeth, later Queen Elizabeth II, riding her tricycle in a park, 1935
Top right: Princess Elizabeth (R) and Princess Margaret playing with tent ropes at a fair in Scotland, 1933
Bottom right: King George VI and Queen Elizabeth with Princesses Margaret Rose (L) and Elizabeth at Y Bwthyn Bach, presented to the Princesses by the people of Wales, 1936

Princess Elizabeth, alongside Princess Margaret, attended their parents' coronation in Westminster Abbey on 12 May 1937. The ceremony had originally been planned for King Edward VIII. As the little girl watched her father and mother receive their crowns by the Archbishop of Canterbury, she understood it would one day be her turn.

Still, the new King and Queen were determined to provide their daughters with as normal an upbringing as possible under the circumstances.

Her father would occasionally provide tuition, as would Henry Martin, the Vice-Provost of Eton. The Archbishop of Canterbury also offered occasional religious instruction. Her schooling was mostly comfortable, sheltered and pleasant. Although she really only had her little sister for competition.

Teachers recall her being especially fond of history, music and languages. She learnt French from a variety of French and Belgian governesses, and became so fluent that the language would later serve her well as Queen when visiting French speaking countries as well as French-Canada.

To allow her to interact with other girls of similar age, Elizabeth's parents decided to enrol her in Girl Guides. This is an organisation run along similar lines to The Boy Scouts Association, aiming to provide children with an education in outdoor activity.

The British Royal Family had close links to Girl Guiding in the United Kingdom. Princess Elizabeth's aunt, Princess Mary, had been President of the Association in 1920. So in 1937 there was no hesitation in providing Princess Elizabeth with the Girl Guides experience. She joined the 1st Buckingham Palace Unit. This had been specially set up within Buckingham Palace, and featured around 20 young girls who were children of members of the Royal Household as well as some palace employees.

They first met on 9 June, with Princess Elizabeth

elected second of the Kingfisher Patrol. Patricia Mountbatten, Elizabeth's third cousin, was elected Patrol Leader. The group met at a summerhouse in the garden. The outbreak of the Second World War and subsequent bombing of London forced the group to cancel meetings for a few years, until it was decided Windsor Castle was safe enough for meetings again in 1942.

To ensure Princess Margaret didn't feel left out, a Brownie Pack was also formed at Buckingham Palace. It contained 14 members.

King George and Queen Elizabeth with Princesses Elizabeth (centre) and Margaret and members of the extended Royal Family in full Coronation regalia on the balcony of Buckingham Palace after their Coronation ceremony.

H R H Princess Elizabeth and Philip Mountbatten, Duke of Edinburgh, on the occasion of their engagement at Buckingham Palace in London, 1947

THE PRINCESS MEETS HER LOVE

A 1939 visit to the Royal Naval College at Dartmouth would prove very fateful for thirteen year old Princess Elizabeth.

While King George VI and Queen Elizabeth toured the grounds and performed their royal duties, somebody was needed to mind Princesses Elizabeth and Anne.

Earl Mountbatten suggested his nephew, Philip.

A member of the House of Schleswig-Holstein-Sonderburg-Glucksberg, Philip was born in Corfu, Greece on 10 June 1921. He was the fifth and final child (and only son) of Prince Andrew of Greece and Denmark and Princess Alice of Battenberg.

In September 1922, things had gone very sour for his family in Greece. Philip's uncle, King Constantine I, had to abdicate and the military government arrested his father Prince Andrew. Three months later a military court banished Prince Andrew from Greece for the remainder of his life. With his family, they left aboard the HMS *Calypso*, baby Philip carried in a cot made from a fruit box. They travelled to France and started a new life in the Paris suburb of Saint-Cloud.

Prince Philip received education in France, England, Germany and Scotland, before joining the British Naval Academy at age 18.

It was at this point in his life that he met Princess Elizabeth. He had finished at the Gordonstoun school in Moray, Scotland earlier that year and had subsequently joined the Royal Naval College at Dartmouth. So he was on grounds and available to act as chaperone to two young princesses in need of entertaining on that summer day in July, 1939.

And Princess Elizabeth certainly was entertained. Smitten even.

Philip was a third cousin, through the Princess' Great Grandmother Queen Victoria, as well as a second cousin once removed through King Christian IX of Denmark.

A black and white photograph taken that day shows the Prince and two girls sharing a game of croquet.

Elizabeth's nanny, Marion Crawford, recalled that she "never took her eyes off him" though for Philip's part, he didn't pay her any special attention.

Nevertheless, they started exchanging letters. When Philip was called up for war service, Crawford said Elizabeth was incredibly proud to have the privilege of writing to a man who was fighting for Britain.

She began to take more time to get her appearance right, Crawford noticed she would often play the tune "People Will Say We're in Love" from the musical 'Oklahoma'.

After the war ended, Philip remained overseas. He stayed in the Far East with the destroyer Whelp, helping to collect and bring home prisoners of war. He arrived back in Portsmouth on 17 January 1946.

He found the return to the home country a little unsatisfying. In a letter to Princess Elizabeth, Philip admitted he was "still not accustomed to the idea of peace, rather fed up with everything and feeling that there was not much to look forward to and rather grudgingly accepting the idea of going on in the peacetime navy."

But at the very least, his home postings gave him the opportunity to see Princess Elizabeth and to continue courting her. He would often arrive at Buckingham Palace forecourt in a black, green-upholstered MG Sports Car. Marion Crawford remembered him exiting the vehicle "hatless" and "always in a hurry to see Lilibet".

At his place of residence in London (usually either at Kensington Palace with his grandmother Princess Victoria, or at a camp bed at the home of Dickie Mountbatten) he would always keep a photograph of Princess Elizabeth in a battered leather frame close to his bedside.

In dramatic contrast to royal romance in more recent decades, the relationship between Princess Elizabeth and Philip was allowed to blossom largely away from the fixed gaze of the press.

On 26 May 1946, Elizabeth and Philip were photographed together at the wedding of the Princess' new lady-in-waiting. However he was described in the press as "a figure largely unknown to the British public".

The couple took steps not to draw attention to themselves when they were together. If they went to the same party, they took care to not be seen dancing with each other.

That's not to say the relationship went by completely unnoticed, especially by members of the royal household. In fact, there was some opposition to the potential match.

During visits to Balmoral, certain guests found Philip to be "rather unpolished".

His place of education was also a concern, in those days where the status of one's school meant a great deal. Virtually every other potential suitor had

The royal family arriving at the Royal Naval College in Dartmouth. L-R are Prince Philip of Greece, Princess Margaret, Queen Elizabeth, King George VI and Princess Elizabeth, 1939

been educated at Eton College. Philip's Gordonstoun education was seen as dangerously progressive.

He was mocked as being "no gentleman" for his sometimes rude and overbearing manner. His sense of self-reliance came across as cockiness and arrogance.

Then there was the King and Queen. Though George VI and Elizabeth didn't outright oppose the relationship, they had their own misgivings. Diplomat Harold Nicholson recalled how they felt Philip was "rough, ill-mannered, uneducated and would probably not be faithful". Sir Edward Ford recalls Queen Elizabeth coming up with eleven potential suitors for her eldest daughter, "and it's hard to known whom she would have sent in first, but it certainly wouldn't have been Philip".

Fortunately, the more they got to know him, the more the King and Queen came to like him. They began to see what their daughter saw in him.

The attributes that others saw as knocks on Philip's character seemed to attract Princess Elizabeth to him. She loved his forthrightness and his independence, especially in contrast to all the fawning she received from other suitors.

By June of 1946 the relationship began to get more serious. He wrote to the Princess that month, apologising for arriving at Buckingham Palace uninvited, "Yet however contrite I feel there is always a small voice that keeps saying 'nothing ventured, nothing gained' – well I did venture and I gained a wonderful time".

His letters during this time revealed how deeply in love he was falling. He wrote of how the Princess gave his life a purpose, "To have been spared in the war and seen victory, to have been given the chance to rest and to re-adjust myself, to have fallen in love completely and unreservedly, makes all one's personal and even the world's troubles seem small and petty".

In the late summer of 1946, Princess Elizabeth asked him to Balmoral for three weeks of shooting grouse and stalk.

It was at some point in time over the course of that visit that he proposed.

Top: Princess Elizabeth (later Queen Elizabeth II) and Prince Philip of Greece, (later The Duke of Edinburgh) act as Bridesmaid and usher at the wedding of Patricia Mountbatten and Lord Brabourne, 1946

Middle: Princess Elizabeth and her fiancé, Philip Mountbatten at Buckingham Palace, after their engagement was announced, July 10, 1947

Bottom: Princess Elizabeth dances with her fiancé, Philip Mountbatten, in public for the first time at a ball, July 15, 1947

THE SECOND WORLD WAR

In September 1939, in response to the invasion of Poland, Great Britain declared war on Nazi Germany.

When war was declared, King George VI, Queen Elizabeth and the girls had been in Scotland. The King and Queen hurried back to London, but chose to leave the girls behind so that they were out of any immediate harm's way.

They stayed under the close watch of nanny Clara Knight and governess Marion Crawford. The King and Queen hoped that despite all the turmoil and uncertainty of the war, the girls could continue to live as normally as possible.

For the most part, they did. They carried on with their usual lessons, and even joined the local Girl Guide Company for hikes, tea parties and other outings.

To highlight how relaxed the Royal Family were about their security in the early days of war, they even chose to celebrate Christmas in Sandringham, despite the location potentially being a target for German attack from across the North Sea.

In February 1940, the princesses moved to the Royal Lodge in Windsor Great Park.

For some months after the war's beginning, most Londoners weren't directly affected anyway. Those early days were soon dubbed 'the Phony war', as the major powers prepared for largescale battle without engaging in much direct fighting.

That wasn't to last long though. Sure enough, Nazi Germany had a plan to destroy the British war effort, and it involved attacking the capital. The Luftwaffe started its aerial bombardment of London a year later.

Though many of the city's children had already, or were in the process of being evacuated, Princess Elizabeth and her younger sister remained with their parents in London.

A senior politician, Lord Hailsham, had suggested the girls be taken to Canada to get well and truly out of harm's way, however the Queen refused. She famously declared, "The children won't go without me. I won't leave without the King. And the King would never leave".

In the blitz's darkest days, the Royal Family's insistence on remaining in the capital provided a great deal of inspiration and hope to a battered population. Adolf Hitler would go as far as declaring Queen Elizabeth the world's most dangerous woman for her decision to keep the family in London.

That's not to say that Princesses Elizabeth and Margaret stayed right in the thick of things at Buckingham Palace. Even before the Blitz started, they spent Christmas 1939 at Balmoral Castle in Scotland, and for a few weeks after that lived at Sandringham House at

Princesses Elizabeth and Margaret making a broadcast to the children of the Empire during World War II, 1940

*Princess Elizabeth trains
as an ATS mechanic, 1945.*

Norfolk. From February to May 1940 they stayed at the Royal Lodge at Norfolk. Finally they went to Windsor Castle, where they would live for most of the next five years of war.

Even so, the Princesses did whatever they could do to aid the war effort. In 1940, a fourteen year old Elizabeth gave her first ever radio address. She reached out to other children who had been evacuated from the city: "We are trying to do all we can to help our gallant soldiers, sailors and airmen, and we are trying, too, to bear our share of the danger and sadness of war. We know, every one of us, that in the end all will be well."

Three years later, at sixteen years of age, Elizabeth made her first solo appearance. She visited the Grenadier Guards, which she had been appointed colonel of the year before.

As she neared her eighteenth birthday, the British Parliament changed the law to allow her to act as one of five Counsellors of State, in the event of her father's incapacity or absence overseas, such as when he visited Italy in 1944.

As the war lingered on, a plan emerged to use Princess Elizabeth as a way to soften the increasing Welsh nationalism. Politicians in Wales suggested she become the Princess of Wales on her 18th birthday. The Home Secretary liked the idea, however the King did not. He believed the title should remain firmly that of the wife of a Prince of Wales, which itself had always been the title of a male heir apparent.

In February 1945, Elizabeth became a member of the Women's Auxiliary Territorial Service as honorary Second Subaltern. Her service number was 230873. She completed training as a driver and mechanic, and within five months had been promoted to honorary Junior Commander. Her automobile training would serve her well throughout her lifetime, as she became fond of driving cars around her private estates such as Balmoral.

The long war came to an end of 8 May 1945. Adolf Hitler had committed suicide and the Allies were sweeping across what was left of the Third Reich. On the previous day, Germany had surrendered unconditionally at Rheims, and the news was relayed to the world the next day. In London, same as it was all around the Allied world, the reaction was one of sheer jubilation.

Princess Elizabeth certainly wasn't immune to the enthusiasm of an end to a war that had come to dominate her teenage years.

That afternoon and evening of 8 May, large crowds gathered outside the gates of Buckingham Palace. The location, surrounding the Queen Victoria Memorial, had often served as a place where people could celebrate good news with the Royal Family.

After appearing on the palace balcony with her mother, father, younger sister, as well as Prime Minister Winston Churchill, Elizabeth was determined to experience it for herself. She convinced her parents and palace security to allow both herself and Margaret outside the palace walls.

"We asked my parents if we could go and see for ourselves. I remember we were terrified of being recognised... I remember lines of unknown people linking arms and walking down Whitehall, all of us just swept along on a tide of happiness and relief."

Under the close watch of minders, the two girls made their way out the front, where the crowds remained eager to catch another glimpse of the King and Queen. They were to get some help this time, as Elizabeth and Margaret sent word back to the palace that they were out the front and eager to see their parents on the balcony. The King and Queen duly obliged and the girls got to experience a royal balcony appearance from the perspective of a regular Londoner.

Queen Elizabeth II, as Princess
Elizabeth, and her husband the
Duke of Edinburgh, styled Prince
Philip in 1957, on their wedding day

PRINCESS ELIZABETH'S MARRIAGE TO PHILIP

It was the news all the United Kingdom had been waiting for. Their princess, and future Queen, was to be married.

Elizabeth certainly had no shortage of suitors as she came of age. Lady Anne Glenconner remembered, "there was a whole battalion of lively young men". And her mother was certainly in favour of one of her daughter's aristocratic friends, perhaps from a family similar to her own English-Scottish background.

However since that first meeting at the Royal Naval College in Dartmouth, the Princess only had eyes for Philip.

That he was extremely handsome and dashing no doubt helped his cause – six feet tall, blue eyes, blond hair – most women's dream.

The news that Princess Elizabeth and Prince Philip of Greece and Denmark had become engaged was made public on 9 July 1947.

It had actually happened much earlier. Way back in the late summer of 1946 in fact. In the midst of a month-long stay at Balmoral, Philip proposed and Elizabeth accepted right there and then. She didn't even take the time to consult her parents, she was that sure of herself. Still, the King would need to approve but that was never in doubt. The King preferred that the public not learn of the engagement until after Elizabeth's 21st birthday, which would be the following April.

Though most reactions to the news were enthusiastic, there was still some hesitation in some quarters of the British establishment and Royal Family.

First and foremost, they still saw Philip as very much an outsider. A 'foreigner' to be more precise. That was despite having lived in the United Kingdom from a very young age, and even serving in the British navy. Even his Greek background came under scrutiny. The name 'Phil the Greek' stuck, and even today is often repeated in less than complimentary fashion.

What hurt Philip's prospects the most though were the links to Germany. Three of his sisters had married members of the Nazi Party in Germany. In 1937, Philip had been photographed in Germany at the funeral of one of those sisters, Cecile. Also present at the service were ranks of soldiers giving Nazi salutes.

Queen Elizabeth, for one, was not so taken with Philip at the outset. She dubbed him Philip 'the Hun' in reference to his European heritage. Her stance softened over time however, and towards the end of her life she remarked to her biographer Tim Heald that Philip was "an English gentleman".

Left: Princess Elizabeth and Prince Philip, wave to crowds from the balcony of Buckingham Palace following their marriage, November 20, 1947

Right: Princess Elizabeth and Prince Philip in the Bridal coach passing through Parliament Square on their return to Buckingham Palace following their marriage

Undeterred, Philip demonstrated his commitment to his fiancé by renouncing his Greek and Danish titles, converting from Greek Orthodoxy to Anglicanism, and adopting the style Lieutenant Philip Mountbatten – the surname taken from his mother's British family. He also became the Duke of Edinburgh shortly before the wedding, and granted the style 'His Royal Highness'.

He even gave up smoking. He knew how upset Elizabeth was at her father's own addiction to cigarettes, and its impact on his health. By all accounts, Philip simply gave up, cold turkey. His valet, John Dean, who had previously kept him well-stocked with cigarettes, said he managed to do so "suddenly and without any real difficulty".

King George VI consented to the marriage. As under the Royal Marriages Act 1772, this happened in his British Privy Council.

The marriage took place at 11.30am on 20 November 1947 at Westminster Abbey. The newlyweds received around 2,500 wedding gifts sent from all around the world.

Though the ceremony certainly was a lavish occasion befitting a royal wedding, the Princess remained ever-mindful of the hardships affecting Britain. The war had ended just two years earlier, but the country was still experiencing great hardship. Rationing for basic food and supplies was still commonplace. Princess Elizabeth paid for the material used to create her wedding gown from ration coupons. She also did her own make-up.

The dress had been designed by leading British fashion designer Norman Hartnell, whose signature was embroidery. The train was said to symbolise rebirth and growth following the war, and was also inspired by a 1482 Botticelli painting. The dress was decorated with crystals, as well as 10,000 seed pearls, imported from the United States of America.

According to Hartnell, it was "the most beautiful dress I had so far made".

Disaster almost struck with that wedding outfit. As the Princess was getting dressed at Buckingham Palace, her tiara snapped. Fortunately, the court jeweller had been on standby just in case an emergency like this developed. A police escort rushed the jeweller to his work room, and with Queen Elizabeth reassuring her daughter it would be fixed in time for the wedding, it was.

The guest list was notable for who was not there as much as who attended. With the memories of the Second World War still fresh in everyone's minds, it wasn't appropriate for Prince Philip's German relations to attend.

Eight bridesmaids attended to Princess Elizabeth. They were her younger sister Princess Margaret, her first cousin Princess Alexandra of Kent, Lady Caroline Montagu-Douglass Scott, her second cousin Lady Mary Cambridge, Lady Elizabeth Lambart, the Hon. Pamela Mountbatten, her first cousin the Hon. Margaret Elphinstone, and her first cousin the Hon. Diana Bowes-Lyon.

Her cousins Prince William of Gloucester and Prince Michael of Kent served as page boys.

Notably, the former King Edward VIII (now styled Edward, the Duke of Windsor) and his wife Wallis, the Duchess of Windsor, also did not receive an invitation. The Duke and his wife had been living in Paris and were mostly unwelcome back home in the United Kingdom. The Duke also conceded that having a current and former living monarch in the same place would be unprecedented for the United Kingdom and would create all sorts of distraction. His presence wasn't exactly missed either. The Duke had fostered a great deal of mistrust during the war years with his suspected sympathy for Adolf Hitler and Fascism.

Princess Elizabeth and Prince Philip receiving the blessing of the Archbishop of Canterbury as they kneel on the steps of the sanctuary in Westminster Abbey during their wedding ceremony, November 20, 1947

The weather was extremely cold on the wedding day. Nevertheless, tens of thousands of spectators turned out to catch a glimpse of the young couple as well as any other members of the Royal Family and British establishment they could spot.

Princess Elizabeth arrived at Westminster Abbey alongside King George VI in the Irish State Coach.

Following the service, which lasted roughly an hour, the bride and groom led a procession down the nave in front of an audience that included the heads of Norway, Denmark, Romania, Greece and Holland.

Just 150 guests attended the "wedding breakfast" (which was really a luncheon) in the Ball Supper Room. An "austerity menu" featured filet de sole

The Royal family group at the wedding of Princess Elizabeth, and the Duke of Edinburgh, Prince Philip. In the family group are Lord Mountbatten, King George VI, Elizabeth, the Queen Mother, Queen Mary and Princess Margaret Rose.

Mountbatten, perdreau en casserole, and bombe glacée. The wedding cake stood nine feet high, with four tiers, and the newlyweds cut the first slice using Philip's Mountbatten sword.

King George VI, whose health was beginning to decline, chose not to give a major speech. Instead he simply raised a glass of champagne and gave a toast to "the bride."

The Royal Couple were showered with rose petals in the palace forecourt, the newlyweds were transported in an open carriage drawn by four horses to Waterloo Station.

For the honeymoon, the couple spent a week at Broadlands, the Mountbatten estate in Hampshire, as well as two weeks at Birkhall, an 18th century lodge on the Balmoral Estate.

Princess Elizabeth holding her son Prince Charles after his christening ceremony at Buckingham Palace

A NEW PRINCE IS BORN

An excited world waited with baited breath for the birth of a future direct heir to the British throne.

The news that Princess Elizabeth and the Duke of Edinburgh were expecting their first child sent the United Kingdom into a frenzy. It was the middle of 1948, just a few years on from the end of the Second World War. Britain was continuing the long process of rebuilding a society in the post-war aftermath. Rationing continued to be a source of frustration and would continue to be until the early 1950s. So the news that the child that may well be a future King or Queen would be born came as a welcome distraction.

Of course, in those days a boy was the preferred option. The rules of succession for the British throne at the time required a direct male heir to supersede any female heir, even if that female was older. Elizabeth would only become Queen because her father, King George VI, gave birth to two daughters, of which she was the eldest. So while the birth of a daughter would no doubt have been celebrated, it would have been in the knowledge that any future males born to the Queen and King would take precedence. This long-standing tradition would only be abolished well into the 21st century when the Queen's future grandson, Prince William, was expecting a child.

One person however wasn't worried about any such awkward possibility of the child being a girl –

the Duke of Edinburgh. Elizabeth's private secretary Commander John Colville would later admit that while the whole Palace was hopeful for a boy, "Philip was confident".

As the expected delivery date drew closer, an eager nation kept a close eye on the newspapers and radio for word from Buckingham Palace.

'WHOLE WORLD AWAITS BIRTH', cried *The Sunday Mail*.

Even overseas the pregnancy dominated headlines. On the other side of the world Australians also waited impatiently for any news on the arrival of what could one day be their future sovereign. The Courier Mail kept readers up to date with a report that during her final week of pregnancy, Elizabeth had gone for a short walk. The paper noted that both her gynaecologist, Sir William Gilliatt, and Sister Helen Rowe had accompanied her as a precaution.

Just as it was for her mother, Princess Elizabeth's first labour was long. It lasted up to 30 hours, with the Belgian Suite at Buckingham Palace transformed into a temporary maternity ward for the occasion. The room overlooked The Mall, and it would be the first royal birth to take place at Buckingham Palace since Lady Patricia Ramsay, daughter of the first Duke of Connaught, in 1886.

Finally, at around 9.14pm on 14 November 1948 came the news the whole world had been waiting for.

The Princess had given birth to a child. And the Duke was right – it was a boy.

He weighed 7lbs 6oz, which mothers across the country remarked was just about the right weight for a healthy newborn boy.

An extremely pleased Duke of Edinburgh opened a bottle of champagne and, alongside members of his staff, drank to the health of his new child.

Meanwhile, outside the Palace gates, a crowd had been building throughout the preceding days. And since word had filtered throughout the city that the Princess had gone into labour, the throng of people waiting outside had steadily increased.

The Times reported the crowd as quiet at first but with a feeling of subdued excitement. Since it was getting late in the evening for that particular day, they were restless for the news to come through before many would have to head home.

The Daily Telegraph captured the growing excitement as rumours began to spread outside the palace walls, "People in the crowd asked 'Is it true? Is the baby born?' And the officer announced in a loud voice 'Yes you can all go home. A prince has been born'".

It would take until 11.30pm for the official announcement to be made. A gilt frame covered by glass was hung from the palace railings, the signal to the crowd below.

The mood became simply ecstatic, but it was shortlived.

According to *The Guardian*, "The crowds were still cheering at midnight but disappeared soon afterwards in response to an appeal by two officials of the Royal Household who said 'Princess Elizabeth wants to have some rest'".

At 11.55pm a motorcade containing the Princess' grandmother Queen Mary departed the Palace. *The Daily Telegraph* reported, "her car became surrounded by cheering people and forced to a standstill. It could be seen that there were tears in Her Majesty's eyes. She waved and smiled".

On the radio, the BBC broke immediately into scheduled programming to deliver the long awaited announcement to all those Britons not at the Palace. The on-air show was cancelled, with programmers instead choosing to play "suitable records" including Brahms Lullaby and Shepherd's Cradle Song.

The next day, 10 Downing Street released a statement to the press from the UK Cabinet, with all members expressing deep satisfaction at the birth of a son to Princess Elizabeth and the Duke of Edinburgh.

The Guardian, over the next week, reported on the mood right across London, "The flags were out today and few citizens have not heard guns or church bells celebrating the birth of a prince. The news has made people extraordinarily happy. 'Bless her' said a buxom waitress tenderly at luncheon. 'And a boy too'".

Two weeks later, a proud mother sent a letter to her second cousin, Lady Mary Cambridge. "The baby is very sweet, and Philip and I are enormously proud of him. I still find it hard to believe that I really have a baby of my own."

Signing off as 'Lilebet', Elizabeth even noted how hectic the arrival of a young child had made her already busy life, "I had no idea that one could be kept so busy in bed – there seems to be something happening all the time".

The new Prince was baptised on December 15th in the Music Room at Buckingham Palace. Newspapers reported the Holy Water had come straight from the River Jordan.
His godparents were King George VI, Queen Mary, the King of Norway, Princess Margaret, Prince George of Greece and Denmark, the Dowager Marchioness of Milford Haven, the Lady Bradbourne and the Honourable David Bowes-Lyon.

It was also on this day that the world learned of the young Prince's name for the first time – Charles Philip Arthur George.

Main pic: *Princess Elizabeth playing with her son Prince Charles in his private apartments at Buckingham Palace, 1949*

Inset top: *Prince Charles – portrait as a baby*

Inset bottom: *The sponsors of Prince Charles' christening in the music room at Buckingham Palace, December 15, 1948*

The Queen and her retinue walking down the knave of Westminster Abbey after the coronation ceremony

THE PRINCESS BECOMES THE QUEEN

King George VI's health started to seriously decline in the years following the Second World War. The stress of his position during such a time of global crisis, combined with his heavy smoking, had caused his physical condition to steadily deteriorate.

In the late 1940s he developed lung cancer and arteriosclerosis (a hardening of the artery walls, restricting blood flow). His plan to tour Australia and New Zealand in 1949 had to be postponed after suffering an arterial blockage in his right leg, with doctors initially worried he could even lose the limb.

As the new decade rolled around, Princess Elizabeth began to take on more royal duties to alleviate some of the burden from her ailing father.

On 31 January 1952, the Princess departed London travelling to Kenya. She would stay there for a short while before embarking on a longer journey to Australia and New Zealand, having taken her father's place on that postponed tour. Against the wishes of his doctors, The King joined the Princess at Heathrow Airport to wish her well on her journey.

It would be the last time the Princess saw her father alive.

On 6 February 1952, in the early morning hours, King George VI died in bed at Sandringham House in Norfolk. A coronary thrombosis had taken his life at just 56 years of age.

From the moment one British sovereign dies, the next in the line of succession is immediately elevated. Princess Elizabeth was now Queen.

She and the Duke of Edinburgh had just returned to Sagana Lodge, where they had been staying in Kenya, after a night spent at the Treetops Hotel. Once arrived, she received the awful news that her father had passed away overnight. It was her husband that broke the news to her.

Martin Charteris, a courtier, asked the new Queen to choose a regnal name. Though not common among UK royalty, it wasn't unheard of for a new King or Queen to elect to rule under a different name to the one they were born with. Particularly some of the more recent rulers. Her own father was born Albert Frederick Arthur George, but chose to become King George VI.

However the Queen had no such intention. She replied that she would remain Elizabeth "of course". With the first Queen Elizabeth having reigned from 1558 to 1603, the new Queen became Elizabeth II.

To eliminate any confusion, her mother, having been to that point known publicly as Queen Elizabeth, became Elizabeth the Queen Mother.

There was one other thing to clarify regarding the Queen's name. The custom of a wife taking the husband's surname, as well as any children to follow. For the Queen this posed a tricky proposition as to what the name of the royal household should be.

Prime Minister Winston Churchill and Elizabeth's grandmother Queen Mary wanted to keep the 'House of Windsor' name rather than the 'House of Mountbatten' (the Duke of Edinburgh's surname). The Queen ultimately agreed, despite the grumblings from her husband who complained privately he was "the only man in the country not allowed to give his name to his own children." Although in 1960, the Prince would be placated somewhat with the decision to give the surname Mountbatten-Windsor to any male line descendants without royal titles.

Preparations for Elizabeth's coronation began almost immediately. Just as it was for her father, the actual date it would take place would not be for some time as it was considered inappropriate to stage such a lavish celebration straight after the death of the preceding sovereign and during a time of national mourning.

In fact it would take 16 months from the first stages of planning to the actual day of the coronation – 2 June 1953.

Even the death of her grandmother, Queen Mary, in March 1953 would not further delay plans. Queen Mary had expressly stated in her will that her passing should not affect any of the planning for the coronation.

Leading up to the coronation, Elizabeth rehearsed with her maids of honour, using a sheet in place of the long velvet train and an arrangement of chairs acting as a stand-in for the carriage. Two full rehearsals took place on 22 and 29 May.

Of particular difficulty was the Imperial State Crown, which Elizabeth would wear on her head. It was notoriously heavy, so to get accustomed to its weight and feel, she chose to practise wearing it when going about some of her daily activities. This included wearing it at her desk, at tea, and while reading the newspaper.

Above pics: Preparations underway for to celebrate the Coronation of Queen Elizabeth II, 1953

Main pic (opposite page): Queen Elizabeth II arrives at Westminster Abbey in the Coronation Coach wearing her Coronation robes and Sovereign crown. With her are her Maids of Honour and the Duke of Edinburgh, June 2, 1953

Queen Elizabeth II arrives at Westminster Abbey in the Coronation Coach wearing her Coronation robes and Sovereign crown. With her are her Maids of Honour and the Duke of Edinburgh

The day of the coronation was as big a spectacle London had ever seen and as many as three million people were estimated to have gathered on the city streets lining the route of the procession. Stands and scaffolding had been erected in many parts in order to fit so many people and give them a decent view. Many had to camp out overnight to ensure their spot offered a perfect view of the Queen's carriage. They saw sailors, soldiers and airmen from right across the Commonwealth line the route as well.

For anyone not lucky enough to be inside Westminster Abbey, more than 200 microphones had been dotted across the procession, recording what happened inside the famous cathedral.

And it certainly proved a lavish spectacle.

The Lord High Steward of England, Viscount Cunningham of Hyndhope, carried St Edwards Crown into the church.

Then a group of men, led by the Garter Principal King of Arms George Bellew, asked all the audience in each direction, "Sirs, I here present unto you Queen Elizabeth, your undoubted Queen, wherefore all you who are come to this day to do your homage and service, are you willing to do the same?" The crowd replied, "God Save Queen Elizabeth" every time, to which the Queen curtseyed in return.

She received the Armills (bracelets), Stole Royal, Robe Royal and the Sovereign's Orb, as well as the Queen's Ring, the Sceptre with the Cross, and the Sceptre with the Dove.

Once those items were in her hands, the Archbishop of Canterbury, Geoffrey Fisher, took St Edward's Crown, with the crowd shouting "God Save The Queen" three times at the very moment the crown touched her head.

The Abbey then broke into a rendition of 'God Save The Queen'.

Queen Elizabeth II then departed Westminster Abbey through the nave and apse, out the Great West Door, and was followed by members of the Royal Family, the clergy, and ministers of government.

Thousands of military personnel from around the Commonwealth helped to escort her back to Buckingham Palace. Once arrived back at the Palace, the Queen and Prince Philip appeared on the balcony of the Centre Room to wave to the crowds gathered outside as a flypast roared overhead.

The day was an incredible success. And it wasn't just the enthusiasm and big crowds in London that made it so. The coronation was the first ever to be televised, allowing many more around the world to experience the day's proceedings. In Canada, RAF planes were tasked with flying film from the ceremony across the Atlantic Ocean to be broadcast on the Canadian Broadcasting Corporation.

Main pic (top): Queen Elizabeth II on the balcony at Buckingham Palace after her coronation, June 2, 1953

Middle: The royal group in the throne room of Buckingham Palace in honour of the Coronation of Queen Elizabeth II, including the Duke of Edinburgh, Prince Charles, Princess Anne, the Queen Mother, Princess Margaret, the Duke of Gloucester, the Duchess of Gloucester, the Duchess of Kent, June 2, 1953

Bottom: Queen Elizabeth II's coronation procession passes through Marble Arch in London, June 2, 1953

THREE MORE CHILDREN

PRINCESS ANNE

Princess Elizabeth gave birth to her second child two years after her first – on 15 August 1950.

The birth took place late in the morning at Clarence House, a royal residence in London, located on The Mall not far from Buckingham Palace.

This time it was a girl. She weighed exactly 6lb (2.7kg). She was given the name Princess Anne.

The Duke of Edinburgh toasted to his new daughter's health with his staff. He also telephoned King George VI who had been staying at Balmoral Castle. As he was out shooting, a special messenger had to be dispatched to find the King and inform him he had another grandchild.

The world learned of the new royal's birth when signs were posted on the gates of Clarence House, outside the Home Office in Whitehall, and at Mansion House in the city.

At 3.30pm, the Royal Salute was fired in Hyde Park by the King's Troop of the Royal Horse Artillery. Tradition dictated that the case of the first round fired was engraved and sent to Princess Elizabeth.

Even overseas, the news of another young royal made headlines. In Australia, people stood and cheered when the announcement came through at the evening cinemas and theatres. In the United States, radio announcers broke into regular programming, and afternoon newspapers changed their headlines, providing a relief from all the news coming from the war in Korea.

She was baptised in the Music Room at Buckingham Palace. Her godparents were her grandmother Queen Elizabeth; Princess Margarita of Greece and Denmark; Princess Andrew of Greece and Denmark; Louis Mountbatten and Rev the Hon Andrew Elphinstone.

As with other royal children, a governess was appointed to look after the princess and be responsible for her early education. Catherine Peebles, who served as governess for Prince Charles, took on the duty.

To give the Princess a chance to meet and socialise with girls around her age, a Girl Guides Company was re-established. The 1st Buckingham Palace Company, including the Holy Trinity Brompton Pack, reformed in May 1959. This was similar to her own mother's Girl Guides experience as she was growing up. Princess Anne remained an active Girl Guides member until 1963, when she departed for boarding school.

Queen Elizabeth holding little Prince Edward (age 1).
In the company of the Duke of Edinburgh, Prince Charles,
Princess Anne and Prince Andrew (age 4), 1965

PRINCE ANDREW

Becoming Queen, and the subsequent increase in royal duties, including tours to various countries, put the prospect of any more children on the backburner for several years.

But in 1959, Buckingham Palace announced that the Queen was again expecting a child to be born early the following year. And in the Belgian Suite, on 19 February 1960, another son was born. To be named Prince Andrew.

At the time of his birth, Prince Andrew stood second-in-line to the British throne, behind older brother Prince Charles. The rules of succession meant he surpassed his older sister, Princess Anne.

His baptism occurred two months later, on 8 April 1960, in the Music Room at Buckingham Palace. Geoffrey Fisher, the Archbishop of Canterbury, conducted the ceremony. His godparents were the Duke of Gloucester, Princess Alexandra of Kent; the Earl of Euston; the Lord Elphinstone; and Mrs Harold Philips.

Andrew's birth was particularly noteworthy as he was the first child born to a reigning monarch at Buckingham Palace since Queen Victoria gave birth to Princess Beatrice in 1856. Andrew would later name his eldest daughter Beatrice.

Just as she did after the birth of Prince Charles, Queen Elizabeth II sent a letter to her second cousin Lady Mary Cambridge. In it, the Queen doted over her new son.

"The baby is adorable, and is very good and putting on weight well. Both the older children are completely riveted by him, and all in all, he's going to be terribly spoilt by all of us, I'm sure!"

Again, a governess was appointed and responsible for his early education. He also attended Heatherdown School, a male preparatory school near Ascot. In 1973, he began education at Gordonstoun, the same school where both his father and older brother had studied.

The royal family in the gardens of Windsor Castle, 1965

PRINCE EDWARD

The Queen's fourth and final child arrived on 10 March 1964. It was another boy, making it three sons and a daughter.

A crowd of people were filmed milling outside the gates of Buckingham Palace for the news. A small notice placed on the gates let them know a boy had been born.

That it was another boy came as a bit of a surprise to the Queen. As her pregnancy progressed, Elizabeth became more and more convinced she was having another daughter. It got to the point where she hadn't even considered any male names.

This was also the only birth that Prince Philip was actually present in the room for.

The birth of another boy meant another shuffling of the line of succession. Prince Edward became third-in-line to the throne, behind older brothers Prince Charles and Prince Andrew.

Prince Edward was baptised on 2 May 1964 in Windsor Castle's Private Chapel by the Dean of Windsor, Robin Woods.

His godparents were Prince Richard of Gloucester, the Duchess of Kent, Princess George William of Hanover, the Prince of Hesse and by Rhine, and the Earl of Snowdon.

Just as it was with his older brothers and sister, a governess looked after him and was mostly responsible for his early education at Buckingham Palace.

Those at Buckingham Palace recall him being a quiet child, whose favourite activities included listening to Terry Wogan on Radio 2, and enjoying the Swedish band ABBA.

At the age of seven, Prince Edward was educated at Gibbs School, before attending Heatherdown School, near Ascot. And just as it was for his father and older brothers, he also studied at Gordonstoun in Scotland.

Though receiving only average grades, he went on to study university at Cambridge, making him just the fourth of five members of the Royal Family to have received a university degree.

Following his graduation, there was some controversy over his next career moves. He joined the Royal Marines as an officer cadet. This was because his university education came with the help of a £12,000 sponsorship from the Marines on condition of future service. However in January 1987 he dropped out of the gruelling commando course. This decision prompted a bit of public criticism, but the worst came from his father. It was reported that Prince Philip gave his son such a berating that he reduced him to tears.

Prince Edward went on to pursue a career in film and television production, before taking up more royal duties as he got older.

Queen Elizabeth II holding a camera at the Olympic Horse Trials at Badminton, whilst Princess Margaret sits behind her, smoking a cigarette and watching the action. Also in the group is Group Captain Peter Townsend (standing left), 1955

ANOTHER MARRIAGE CRISIS

PRINCESS MARGARET AND PETER TOWNSEND

In the weeks and months following the death of King George VI, the Queen's sister Princess Margaret was inconsolable. So grief-stricken by the loss of her father was she, the 21 year old had to be prescribed sedatives to help her sleep at night.

Alongside her widowed mother, Princess Margaret left Buckingham Palace and took up residence at the nearby Clarence House. The new Queen and her family did the opposite, moving from Clarence House to Buckingham Palace.

To assist Elizabeth the Queen Mother, Peter Townsend was appointed Comptroller of her household.

He had met Princess Margaret previously, when she was just 13 years old, when he was in service to King George VI. Observers at the time said it was not really a matter of 'love at first sight'. After all, Peter Townsend was at that point 29 years old and had been married for two and a half years. He was reported to be quite sharp with Princess Margaret, viewing her as no more than a privileged schoolgirl.

But things changed as she grew older, and by 1953, Townsend and Princess Margaret had fallen in love. He proposed marriage.

However he was sixteen years older than her and, more importantly, a divorcee (including having had two children from that previous marriage).

It put Queen Elizabeth II in a rather uncomfortable position. Margaret informed her older sister of the marriage proposal and her intention to say yes. Under the Royal Marriages Act 1772, the Queen had to give consent to the marriage at that point in time, as Margaret was placed far enough up the royal line of succession.

However the memories of 1936, and all the upheaval created by King Edward VIII's abdication and his marriage to Wallis Simpson still lingered in the memories of those at the royal household. In 1950s Britain, society had not evolved enough for another high-ranking royal to marry a divorcee with absolutely no objection from anyone.

The relationship between the pair started to gather more public attention at her sister's coronation. Photographs showed the group captain and Princess Margaret together, laughing and beaming at each other. She was also spotted brushing some fluff off his suit, further setting tongues wagging.

Queen Mary had also recently died, further preoccupying Queen Elizabeth II. And there was the prospect of a royal tour around the Empire for six months following the coronation. It gave the Queen enough reason to ask her sister to wait a while.

In answer to her sister's request for marriage, she replied, "Under the circumstances, it isn't unreasonable for me to ask you to wait a year".

In the meantime, the Queen's private secretary suggested Townsend be reassigned from the Queen

Left: Princess Margaret and Group Captain Peter Townsend, leaving Windsor Castle, 1952

Right: Group Captain Peter Townsend in Brussels, 1952

Mother's household to overseas. She saw the merit in some of that idea, moving him away from Clarence House and into her own.

Still the issue lingered. Princess Margaret was in love.

Just as it was 17 years earlier, the British Cabinet flat-out refused to approve the marriage. The saga dominated news headlines with newspapers reporting the government viewed the marriage as "unthinkable" and that it "would fly in the face of Royal and Christian tradition".

Winston Churchill told the Queen that other Prime Ministers in the Dominions (such as Canada and Australia) were also unanimously against the marriage. And the UK Parliament would never approve it, since the Church of England wouldn't recognise it.

All this wasn't to say that the entire United Kingdom was unanimously against the Princess' intentions. In fact, the people were very sympathetic to her situation. Newspaper polls actually showed more of the public supporting her being able to make this personal choice, even in spite of all the opposition from Church and Government.

Upon her 25th birthday, in August 1955, Princess Margaret was no longer bound to do what her sister told her. The *Royal Marriages Act* at least gave her that much freedom. But she still had to contend with the parliament who needed to sign off on the marriage, as well as the Church who would need to perform the service and make the union official. The Princess simply couldn't ignore that. And they made it clear that if she wanted to marry Peter Townsend, Princess Margaret, as with her uncle before her, would have to renounce her rights to the throne.

She would also have to give up her royal rights and income, as well as being forced to leave England, and potentially having to stay away for as long as five years.

Finally, she made her decision. She would not go through with the marriage.

She issued a statement, written in pencil for her by Group Captain Townsend.

Her statement read:

"I would like it known that I have decided not to marry Group Captain Peter Townsend. I have been aware that, subject to my renouncing my rights of succession, it might have been possible for me to contract a civil marriage. But mindful of the Church's teachings

that Christian marriage is indissoluble, and conscious of my duty to the Commonwealth, I have resolved to put these considerations before others.
I have reached this decision entirely alone, and in doing so I have been strengthened by the unfailing support and devotion of Group Captain Townsend."

The couple separated.

Group Captain Townsend would later move to Belgium, before finally settling in France.

Always a shy, private man, he rarely spoke about his relationship with Princess Margaret in the following years. However he did address it in 1978, in his autobiography *Time and Chance*.

"She could have married me only if she had been prepared to give up everything – her position, her prestige, her privy purse. I simply hadn't the weight, I knew it, to counterbalance all she would have lost."

In 1959, Townsend married Marie Luce Jamagne, a Belgian woman that some observers couldn't help but note bore a strong resemblance to Margaret.

For her part, Princess Margaret would marry photographer Anthony Armstrong-Jones, later known as Lord Snowden. She would have two children with him, however it was not an easy marriage. They would eventually file for divorce.

Princess Margaret and Peter Townsend kept in contact sporadically. They would exchange letters from time to time.

In June 1995, Peter Townsend died at the age of 80. Princess Margaret was reported to have been saddened to hear of her former partner's death.

Princess Margaret and Antony Armstrong-Jones in the grounds of Royal Lodge after they announced their engagement

*Queen Elizabeth II and Prince Philip
during their royal tour of New Zealand, 1977*

1977 – QUEEN ELIZABETH II'S SILVER JUBILEE

The 25th anniversary of Queen Elizabeth II's accession to the throne came in 1977. Not since Queen Victoria, in 1862, had a British royal been sovereign for this long. And unlike that occasion more than a hundred years earlier, the nation was this time in a mood to celebrate (back then, Queen Victoria's husband, Prince Albert, had died a year earlier, devastating the Queen and making any Silver Jubilee celebrations simply out of the question).

The celebrations for Queen Elizabeth II included large scale parties and parades throughout the United Kingdom and Commonwealth. This culminated with the official 'Jubilee Days' in June, to coincide with the official Queen's Birthday holiday.

There were two sets of celebrations earlier in the year also; the proper anniversary was commemorated in church services across the country on 6 February 1977 and continued throughout the month.

The Queen chose to spend that anniversary weekend at Windsor Castle with her family.

Just as it is with the Queen's Birthday celebrations, the rest of the United Kingdom would get a chance to publicly celebrate the occasion during the summer.

Before that however, the Queen and Prince Philip chose to spend much of the early months of that year travelling to various parts of the United Kingdom and Commonwealth to celebrate the Silver Jubilee with people at home and abroad. In total they visited 36 countries, with the estimated distance travelled coming in at 56,000 miles.

It started with record crowds having gathered to see the Royals in Glasgow, Scotland in May. They then journeyed throughout England, including one incredible day in Lancashire where a record one million spectators greeted the couple. A visit to Northern Ireland wrapped up this leg of the Queen's travels.

Later in the summer the Queen and Prince Philip travelled overseas. They went to the Pacific Island nations of Fiji and Tonga. Then it was off to Australia and New Zealand.

Finally, the royal couple made their way over to Canada, with Prince Charles having also travelled across the Atlantic to join his mother and father and greet the crowds. Prince Charles also received a Canadian Silver Jubilee Medal, an award which is now presented by governments to citizens who have made significant contributions to their communities.

On 4 May, both Houses of Parliament presented addresses to the Queen. In her reply she stressed the unity of the nation.

On 6 June, the Queen ignited a bonfire beacon at Windsor Castle. The light emanating from this beacon spread across the night as other bonfire beacons were also ignited in a chain that spread across the whole country.

The following day, crowds lined the route of the procession to St Paul's Cathedral, where the royal family attended a Service of Thanksgiving.

The royals joined a procession down The Mall, with an estimated one million people lining the pavements to see the Royal Family wave to onlookers as they went past in their horse-drawn carriages. It's estimated that a massive 500 million people around the Commonwealth watched the day's events on live television.

Dressed in pink, the Queen and Prince Philip led the procession in the golden state coach.

Even though it had rained overnight, thousands had camped out in order to catch a better view of the procession as it made its way down The Mall, through Trafalgar Square, Fleet Street and Ludgate Hill.

At the Thanksgiving Service, they were joined by the then UK Prime Minister James Callaghan as well as all the living former Prime Ministers (Harold MacMillan, Sir Harold Wilson, Alec Douglas-Home and Edward Heath). And there were many other international leaders there, such as US President Jimmy Carter.

The ceremony began with the Ralph Vaughan Williams arrangement of the hymn "All the people on earth do dwell". This was the same song that played at the Queen's coronation.

Following the service, the Queen and guests attended a lunch in the Guildhall hosted by the Lord Mayor of the City of London Peter Vanneck. She spoke at the reception.

"When I was twenty-one I pledged my life to the service of our people and I asked for God's help to make good that vow. Although that vow was made in my salad days, when I was green in judgment, I do not regret nor retract one word of it."

She would later appear alongside her family on the balcony at Buckingham Palace. The masses of people below delighted and waving Union Jack flags. Joining Her Majesty on the balcony that day

Above pics: Celebrations underway for the Silver Jubilee of Queen Elizabeth II, England, 1977

Crowd hailing Queen Elizabeth II in her gilded state coach during her Silver Jubilee procession, June 1, 1977

were Elizabeth the Queen Mother, Prince Andrew, Princess Margaret, Prince Philip, Lord Louis Earl of Mountbatten, Princess Anne, Prince Edward, and Prince Charles.

This was also the designated day the entire United Kingdom celebrated. Towns and villages of all sizes hosted parties in local streets and civic buildings celebrating the Queen's achievement. Bunting hung from many streets, decorated in the red, blue and white of the United Kingdom flag. Many streets also decorated motor vehicles, depicting historical events in the country's past, and drove them around town.

Two days later, on 9 June, the Queen travelled down the River Thames, from Greenwich to Lambeth, aboard a boat. This re-enacted the famous journeys made by her earlier namesake Queen Elizabeth I.

On this day, the Queen also presided over a fireworks display and took part in a procession of lighted carriages to Buckingham Palace, where she once again greeted onlookers from her balcony.

The Jubilee celebrations weren't without controversy. A punk band called 'The Sex Pistols'

outraged royalists with a series of provocative anti-monarchy messages over the course of the Jubilee. They had released a re-worded version of 'God Save the Queen' with inflammatory lyrics, which BBC Radio refused to play. On Jubilee Day, they tried to sail a boat down the Thames River playing the song, and were arrested as they exited the vessel.

The Sex Pistols were a minority however and not all pop-culture treated the occasion as a negative. In fact, most of Britain was supportive of the Queen and her time as their ruler.

Popular soap opera Coronation Street wrote a Jubilee storyline into the TV series. An elaborate parade was portrayed, with Rovers' Return Inn manageress Annie Walker dressing up as Queen Elizabeth I.

The Jubilee would also have a lasting impact on London. An under-construction section of the Underground train line was renamed the Jubilee Line (it would eventually open in 1979). Other locations to be named in honour of these celebrations were the Silver Jubilee Walkway, and the Jubilee Gardens on the South Bank.

*The Wedding of The Prince
and Princess Of Wales at
St Paul's Cathedral in London,
July 29, 1981*

PRINCE CHARLES MARRIES LADY DIANA SPENCER

Prince Charles had known Lady Diana Spencer for several years.

He first took serious interest in her as a potential bride during the summer of 1980, when they were guests at a country weekend. She watched him play polo, and the two began to fall in love.

As their relationship blossomed, he invited her for a sailing weekend to Cowes aboard the royal yacht Britannia. He then followed this up with an invitation to Balmoral Castle, the Scottish home of the Windsors, to meet his family.

Diana was well-received by the Queen, Prince Philip and the Queen Mother. The Queen was especially relieved to see her eldest son enjoying the company of a woman that wasn't Camilla Parker Bowles. She was married at the time to the Guards Officer Andrew Parker Bowles.

Diana's cause was also helped by the fact she was already well-known to the Royal Family since childhood. Her father, Earl Spencer, had rented a ten-bedroom farmhouse on the Sandringham Estate.

The Queen actually went as far as to help shield Lady Diana from the press, who became increasingly aware of Prince Charles' affections for his new girlfriend, and that she might actually become the one he ended up marrying.

After about six months of official dating, Prince Charles proposed to Diana on 3 February 1981 in the nursery at Windsor Castle. He was 32 years old while his bride-to-be was just 20.

As Diana had a holiday planned for the next week, Charles had hoped she would use the time away to consider his proposal and come back to him with an answer. But Diana had no such thoughts or hesitations and agreed to marry Charles. However their engagement was kept quiet for a few weeks.

It became official on 24 February 1981. Diana chose an elegant ring worth around £30,000. It featured 14 solitaire diamonds surrounding a 12-carat blue Ceylon sapphire set in 18-karat white gold.

The big day came on 29 July 1981. The day had been declared a national holiday, allowing most in the United Kingdom the day off to watch and enjoy the ceremony.

It was a lavish and well-attended occasion. Around 3,500 guests were at St Paul's Cathedral to watch Britain's future King marry.

Charles and Diana decided to hold the wedding at St Paul's, as opposed to Westminster Abbey, which was the traditional venue for royal weddings, because St Paul's allowed for more seating and provided the opportunity for a longer procession through the streets of London, meaning more people would have the chance to catch a glimpse of the happy couple and other members of the royal family.

As many as 600,000 people are estimated to have filled the streets on that summer day, eager to see the beautiful bride and dashing groom.

It was a traditional Church of England service, presided over by the Most Reverend Robert Runcie, the Archbishop of Canterbury.

Lady Diana's entrance was simply stunning. She arrived almost on time for the 11.20am service, having made the journey to St Paul's Cathedral on board the Glass Coach, accompanied by her father Earl Spencer.

It took her three-and-a-half minutes to walk up the aisle. Her dress featured a 25ft train, ivory taffeta and antique lace and had been valued at around £9,000.

She couldn't help but be a bit nervous, which showed through just a little bit when she managed to mix up the Prince's names – calling him Philip Charles Arthur George, rather than Charles Philip. But she wasn't alone there. Prince Charles also muddled some lines – referring to "thy goods" rather than "my worldly goods".

Lady Diana's vows actually caused a bit of a stir at the time. The couple had decided not to have her promise to "obey", which was part of the traditional wording.

Following the private signing ceremony, the newly married couple walked back down the aisle to the refrain from Elgar's 'Pomp and Circumstance'.

As many as 750 million people are believed to have watched the ceremony around the world, and this figure increased upwards to around a billion people when factoring in the radio audience. It was dubbed "the wedding of the century".

Following the ceremony, the newly married couple and 120 guests returned to Buckingham Palace for a wedding breakfast.

There were 27 wedding cakes throughout the day. The official cake had been created by the Naval Armed Forces. It took head baker David Avery 14 weeks to create the cake, and he made two of them, just in case one became damaged.

Diana and Charles then made an appearance on the balcony of Buckingham Palace at around 1.10pm. The crowd below cheered their appreciation when the Prince leaned in and gave his new wife a kiss.

As for the Queen, she was absolutely thrilled with how the whole event had gone. The evening following the wedding, she took some time to watch the day's events all over again on a large television screen in Claridge's that had been specially set up. She pointed delightedly whenever the cameras showed her, and beamed with pleasure when the cameras showed her new daughter-in-law. She didn't leave Claridge's until 1.30am, remarking as she said her goodbyes, "I'd love to stay and dance all night".

Unfortunately the relationship between the Queen and Princess Diana would become more strained as the years progressed. Elizabeth II was at the outset a huge supporter of her new daughter-in-law. Realising just how young and vulnerable Diana was to the life of a royal, she looked at her daughter-in-law as a "new girl" who needed time to get used to things.

But Diana continued to struggle with all the attention that came with becoming the Princess of Wales. The marriage would also come under severe strain as both husband and wife had affairs. Their eventual separation and divorce would be bitter, and much to the Queen's dismay it would be played out in the national media.

Princess Diana and Prince Charles of Wales wave to the crowd from their carriage following their wedding ceremony, July 29, 1981

Prince Charles laughing with his sons in Kensington Palace

TWO GRANDSONS ARE BORN

PRINCE WILLIAM

Prince Charles and Princess Diana's first child was born on 21 June 1982.

At approximately 9.03pm at St Mary's Hospital in London, the Princess of Wales gave birth to a boy weighing 7lbs 1.5oz (3.22kg).

The Princess had gone into labour a few days before her expected delivery date. Once it became clear the baby was on its way, Prince Charles had to cancel a planned match of polo he had scheduled for the Sunday afternoon.

When it was time to go to the hospital, Diana and Charles were accompanied by bodyguards. They shielded the couple from the press, as well as the crowds that would gather in greater numbers as news spread.

The Queen soon heard the news and was said to be delighted. She decided to continue with her scheduled program for that day, which was inspecting the RAF regiment on their 40th anniversary at Wittering in Cambridgeshire.

As television cameras captured the reactions of the crowds outside the hospital, many people told reporters that they would be happy for either a boy or girl to be born. But a majority did favour the birth of a boy.

The labour period was long. After the Princess was admitted she endured 16 hours of it until she successfully gave birth. And it was a boy.

After the child had been born, and both he and mother were safe and well, Prince Charles rang the Queen from the hospital. Elizabeth II was reported to be absolutely delighted, while the Queen Mother was also overjoyed. The good news was also relayed to younger brother Prince Andrew who was serving in the South Atlantic Task Force.

The new father also headed outside the hospital to share the good news and have a chat with the throng of media that had been waiting nearby.

He told them, "I was immensely relieved when it was all over. The Princess was well and the baby's looking lovely. It's marvellous, he's not bad".

Upon being told that the crowds outside had been chanting "Nice one Charlie, let's have another one", the Prince laughed and added, "Bloody hell, give us a chance!"

The world was eager to learn the new prince's name, but Prince Charles stayed tight-lipped on that one,

"We have thought of one or two names, there's a bit of an argument over it".

The Queen would visit her new grandson the following morning, alongside Princess Diana's parents.

Prince Charles also took the time to have another chat with the press waiting outside the hospital, remarking his son was "in excellent form, thank goodness – and looking a bit more human this morning".

Later that day, the world would get its first glimpse of the new baby boy as Diana carried him in her arms and Prince Charles escorted her to a waiting car, to head back to Kensington Palace.

It would take one whole week for news on what the young boy's name would be.

As with any other newborn, choosing the name is entirely a personal choice made by the mother and father in British royalty. But that didn't stop the world from speculating as to what name they might go for.

London betting firm William Hill took quite a lot of money on the name (though it wouldn't reveal exactly how much). The bookies' favourite was George, followed by Louis, Arthur and Philip.

On 28 June, the royal family announced the child had been given the name William Arthur Philip Louis – Prince William for short.

Prince Harry and Prince William sit together on the steps of Highgrove House wearing army uniforms, 1986

There had been four previous Williams who went on to become King. The most recent being King William IV who reigned from 1830 to 1837.

Prince William's birth had been all the more special as he was the first child born to parents who had the titles Prince and Princess of Wales since Prince John way back in 1905.

The baptism ceremony took place in the Music Room at Buckingham Palace on 4 August 1982. This coincided with the 82nd birthday of William's great-grandmother, Elizabeth the Queen Mother. Archbishop of Canterbury Robert Runcie took charge of proceedings, just as he did with William's parents' wedding.

During his toddler years, Prince William was affectionately known as "Wombat" by his parents.

Princess Diana and Prince Charles with Prince William (back) and Prince Harry (front) at Highgrove, 1986

PRINCE HARRY

A little over two years later, on 15 September 1984 at approximately 4.20pm, Charles and Diana added another boy to their family.

Once again, at St Mary's Hospital, Diana gave birth to a child weighing 6lbs 14oz (3.12kg).

In the days leading up to the birth, the British Press reported that both Charles and Diana were hoping for the child to be a girl. Even so, once the boy had been born, both parents were ecstatic.

A Buckingham Palace spokesman would later tell the Press of how Prince Charles rushed to the telephone as soon as the child was safely born. He phoned his mother, the Queen, to inform her of the good news. Elizabeth II had been vacationing with other members of the royal family at Balmoral in Scotland.

Prince Charles again took the time to appear before the estimated 400 strong cheering crowds and media who had gathered outside the hospital. Beaming from ear to ear, he told the happy onlookers that the baby has pale blue eyes and hair of "an indeterminate colour".

When asked about how the Princess was doing, Charles responded "my wife is well". He added, "the delivery couldn't have been better. It was much quicker this time than last time".

He thanked them for their well-wishes and support, and joked that they nearly had a full polo team now. He admitted it was time to head off for a "stiff drink".

1992 – THE ANNUS HORIBILIS

I f ever Queen Elizabeth II, and her family, had a year they would prefer to forget, it came in 1992. This was a year which in looking back upon, the Queen came up with the phrase "Annus Horibilis" to describe how she felt about it. It was such a bad year for her, that it would be one of the few times throughout her reign that she felt compelled to discuss her family's private life with the public. And this was from a woman famous for keeping a stoic frame of mind, and not letting the public see her own personal feelings on things.

It started in March, when her second son, Andrew, the Duke of York, announced he would be separating from his wife, Sarah, the Duchess of York. A distressing event in itself as the Queen saw her child's marriage crumble, but then she had to endure the indignity of the Press and how they responded to the breakdown of that marriage. The tabloids were all over the salacious details. They would publish scandalous photographs of the Duchess of York topless and being kissed on the feet by her friend John Bryan.

In April, another of her children's marriages officially ended. Princess Anne and Captain Mark Philips announced they would be divorcing.

In May, Diana, the Princess of Wales released her tell-all book, *Diana, Her True Story*.

Despite plenty of whispers and innuendo throughout the 1980s, the Press chose to withhold reports of disquiet between Prince Charles and Princess Diana. This was mostly out of respect for the Queen who had gone as far as to speak with tabloid editors asking them to let her son and daughter-in-law be able to work out their differences in peace.

But even so, rumours had been swirling that the relationship between Prince Charles and Princess Diana had been deteriorating. However as it became increasingly obvious that the couple were growing further apart, the story began to get bigger and bigger.

It all culminated in May 1992, with the release of the book, authored by Andrew Moreton. Within it, the secrets of the Princess' difficult life as a member of the royal family were laid bare. It talked of her unhappiness, which had driven her to the brink of suicide. It also exposed affairs on both sides. Prince Charles had resumed his relationship with Camilla Parker Bowles, while Diana had been seeing Major James Hewitt.

In the following months, the press published transcripts of intimate conversations between Diana and James Gibley. Later in the year, transcripts were also released of embarrassing conversations between Prince Charles and Camilla.

All this irreparably harmed the Prince and Princess of Wales' marriage and they were divorced within a few years.

Finally, in November, Windsor Castle caught fire. As one of the Queen's residences, the building held

*Queen Elizabeth II making
her 'Annus Horribilis' speech –
describing her sadness at the
events of the year which included
the marriage breakdown of two
of her sons and the devastating
fire at her home Windsor Castle,
November 24, 1992*

Top: Duke And Duchess Of York with their children Princess Beatrice and Princess Eugenie at Royal Windsor Horse Show after their official separation

Middle: Princess Anne with her children, Zara and Peter Phillips, and members of staff

Bottom: Prince Charles and Princess Diana on their last official trip together - a visit to the Republic of Korea (South Korea)

a special place in Her Majesty's heart and it saddened her to see it so seriously damaged. Not to mention the priceless artefacts lost.

The fire simply came at the wrong time. Any other year and the question of costs may not have raised many eyebrows at all. But the damaging scandals embroiling the royal family were seriously hurting their credibility. Republican sentiment, though still small within the United Kingdom, was starting to make some headway. To put it simply, people were fed up with this family dominating news headlines in a way that did not reflect well on the country they represented.

So the fire opened up a serious debate within Britain over just how much money the public were expected to pay to repair Windsor Castle. In effect, it became an argument over just how much money the Queen and her family expected from the taxpayer.

Prime Minister John Major had initially indicated the government would fully cover the cost of repairs. However this was met with stiff resistance. Politicians took advantage of the negative response and complained publicly that as the Queen was worth anywhere between $135 million to $9 billion, she should be forced to pay at least part of the expenses. Especially since she also paid no income tax.

In the end, a compromise was reached, with the government opening some of the publicly owned royal residences to tourists during the summer when the Queen would not be in residence, and the revenue from this would go towards the Windsor Castle repairs.

The fire occurred four days before the Queen was due to speak to the Guidhall on 24 November 1992.

With the debate over costs fresh in her mind, and in addition to everything else that had happened over the course of the year, the Queen chose to use the speech to deliver a rather unprecedented admission of the difficulties of her role and how her family's struggles had affected her. For the first time, she also touched on the role the British public played in her life.

Another disaster in the Queen's "Annus Horribilis" speech when a fire broke out at Windsor Castle – a tragedy damaging more than 100 rooms

It became famously known as her *Annus Horribilis* speech.

"I suspect that I am not alone in thinking it so. Indeed, I suspect that there are very few people or institutions unaffected by these last months of worldwide turmoil and uncertainty. This generosity and whole-hearted kindness of the Corporation of the City to Prince Philip and me would be welcome at any time, but at this particular moment, in the aftermath of Friday's tragic fire at Windsor, it is especially so.

"I sometimes wonder how future generations will judge the events of this tumultuous year. I dare say that history will take a slightly more moderate view than that of some contemporary commentators. Distance is well-known to lead enchantment, even to less attractive views. After all, it has the inestimable advantage of hindsight.

"But it can also lead an extra dimension to judgment, giving it a leavening of moderation and compassion – even of wisdom – that is sometimes lacking in the reactions of those whose task it is in life to offer instant opinions on all things great and small.

"There can be no doubt, of course, that criticism is good for people and institutions that are part of public life. No institution – City, Monarchy – whatever – should expect to be free from the scrutiny of those who give it their loyalty and support, not to mention those who don't.

"But we are all part of the same fabric of our national society and that scrutiny, by one part or another, can be just as effective if it is made with a touch of gentleness, good humour and understanding."

Immediately following the speech, reactions were rather mixed.

Conservative politician Patrick McNair Wilson praised the Queen's "personal courage" in a difficult year.

But some Labour MPs couldn't help but point out there was no offer to pay for any of Windsor Castle's repairs.

Most detractors did concede however that these sort of candid remarks into the personal lives of her family was unusual for the Queen, especially in such a public setting. They admired her bravery. It showed she was prepared to acknowledge the criticisms of the monarchy, though maybe not necessarily agree with them.

And it also gave her an opportunity to show humility and to plead for understanding.

Prince Charles, Prince Harry, Earl Spencer, Prince William and the Duke of Edinburgh follow the coffin to the funeral cortege of Diana, Princess of Wales as it arrives at Westminster Abbey, September 6, 1997

68

DEATH OF A PRINCESS

In the early hours of 31 August 1997, a single high-speed car crash in a Parisian tunnel stopped the world in its tracks.

Princess Diana had been divorced from Prince Charles for more than two years, and though she still played an active role in the upbringing of their two sons William and Harry, she had become mostly estranged from the remainder of the royal family.

Diana and her new boyfriend Dodi Fayad had flown into Paris via private jet earlier in the day on Saturday 30 August. The plan had been to stop overnight en route to London, having just spent nine days aboard Dodi's father's yacht on the French Riviera.

The pair left Hotel Ritz Paris at 12.20am in a hired black 1994 Mercedes-Benz S280. A decoy vehicle had departed first, the idea being to lure some of the more eager members of the paparazzi away from the couple.

The 'paparazzi' (stemming from an Italian dialect word for a buzzing mosquito) were photographers who made their money snapping candid shots of celebrities. And in the late 90s, Princess Diana was their number one target. Newspapers, magazines and TV news programs all around the world paid good money for images of the Princess of Wales going about her daily life away from the royal family. The best, and most valuable photographs, were those that had Diana with men, which at this point meant Dodi Fayad.

Having spent almost two decades in the public eye, Princess Diana was used to the media's attention, so the presence of the paparazzi on this particular night posed no concern to her. However she and her minders still liked to get them away from her wherever they could, in order to give her and Dodi some moments of peace. So the idea to send off a decoy vehicle, or to have her vehicle travel at fast speeds to get away from the chasing pack was not unusual.

Diana and Dodi's car sped off, towards an apartment in Rue Arsene Houssaye. They travelled in the back seat of the car. Trevor Rees-Jones, who worked as part of the Fayad family's personal security team, took the front passenger seat. The driver was Henri Paul, the deputy head of security at the Ritz Hotel, who had been given the responsibility of transporting the couple around Paris that night.

The car left rue Cambon and crossed over the Place de la Concorde. They headed along Cours la Reine and Cours Albert, all the while putting further distance between themselves and those members of the paparazzi who had access to motorcycles.

At approximately 12.23am, the car entered the Place de l'Alma underpass – a short tunnel crossing underneath a busy intersection above that marked the entrance to the Pont de l'Alma bridge.

It was at this point that disaster struck. It's never been revealed exactly how it happened. What is known is that Henri Paul lost control of the Mercedes at high speed.

The car veered to the left of the two-lane carriageway, before striking a pillar head-on.

A reconstruction of the crash would reveal the car had reached speeds of 65 mph (105 kilometres) through this tunnel. The vehicle spun and then hit the stone wall of the tunnel backwards before coming to a rest.

It took several moments for the chasing photographers and other witnesses to catch up to the horrific scene. They found the Mercedes substantially damaged, almost beyond recognition.

They found Diana critically injured. Reports later emerged that she kept muttering softly

"Oh my God", and as police attempted to push away bystanders, "Leave me alone".

Dodi Fayad appeared to be dead. Henri Paul was declared dead as soon as his body was pulled from the twisted wreckage. Only Trevor Rees-Jones survived, but he had suffered multiple serious facial injuries.

No-one had been wearing seatbelts.

As emergency workers pulled Diana from the wreckage, she went into cardiac arrest. They managed to get her heart beating again, and she was taken by ambulance to the Pitie-Salpetriere Hospital.

Despite repeated attempts to save her, the internal injuries proved too great for doctors to overcome, and Diana, the Princess of Wales died in hospital at 4.00am.

Main pic: Wreckage of Princess Diana's car in the Alma tunnel in Paris

Inset: Princess Diana (L) and Dodi al Fayed (R) and wreckage of the car in which Diana and al Fayed died in a road accident

Members of the royal family, including The Queen, Prince Philip and Prince Charles, had been staying at Balmoral Castle in Scotland. They were woken in the early hours of 31 August with the news Diana had been involved in a serious accident.

At 4.00am they received the terrible news that she had died. They were now faced with the awful prospect of having to wake her two sons, Prince William and Prince Harry, who were still just children, and tell them their mother was gone.

Meanwhile, moments later the world learned she had died in a press conference featuring a hospital doctor, the French Interior Minister Jean-Pierre Chevenement, and Britain's ambassador to France Sir Michael Jay. News of the crash had already spread across the planet like wildfire.

The death of Princess Diana shocked the world. Whatever people thought of her, she had been a constant presence in global news for almost two decades. Her personal life in particular the subject of intense scrutiny and speculation. As with many celebrities, people felt like they knew her personally.

The tragedy was felt hardest in the United Kingdom, which plunged into an almost unprecedented state of mourning, the likes of which had not been seen in many years. Prime Minister Tony Blair summed up the public's grief when he labelled her the 'People's Princess'. Though Diana did have aristocratic ancestry, people still felt she had been one of them.

Her funeral was held a week later, on 6 September 1997, at Westminster Abbey in London. As many as 3 million people are believed to have lined the streets of London for the procession. It's estimated the television coverage of the service attracted 2.5 billion viewers.

Among the mourners were several notable names including First Lady Hillary Clinton (the wife of United States President Bill Clinton), Bernadette Chirac (the wife of French President Jacques Chirac), Italian tenor Luciano Pavarotti, and singers George Michael and Elton John (the latter three all personal friends of Diana).

One of the service's best moments came when Elton John took to the stage and performed a re-worded version of his song Candle In the Wind, with the lyrics changed to reflect Diana's life ("Goodbye England's rose"). The song rocketed up the music charts in the following days.

Main pic: Newspaper headlines announcing the death of Princess Diana and Dodi Fayed in a car crash in Paris

Inset left: Sir Elton John sings "Candle In The Wind" at the funeral of Diana, Princess of Wales

Inset right: Flowers and tributes outside Kensington Palace

The tragedy would again bring the royal family under severe scrutiny. It would develop into one of the most serious crises the Queen had ever faced.

There was a sense of anger at how the royal family had pushed Diana away following the divorce (whether true or not).

The public reaction of the Royal Family in the days immediately after her death was also not received very well. In comparison to the immense outpouring of mourning going on elsewhere, the royal family remained rather quiet, preferring to deal with it privately.

Their decision not to immediately end their holiday at Balmoral Castle and return to London provoked much criticism.

However the Queen insisted Diana's two boys, Prince William and Prince Harry, should be allowed to grieve the loss of their mother in private, with their families, and away from the intense glare of the public and media that would no doubt have happened had they all returned to London in the following days.

Another point of contention was the flying of the Royal Standard at Buckingham Palace. Passers-by wondered why there was no flag at all in the days after Diana's death. The popular understanding of flag protocol is that it flies at half-mast upon the death of a notable person. So it was naturally expected that the former Princess of Wales would be honoured in this way. But the flagpole remained bare.

Buckingham Palace's response was that the Standard only flew when The Queen herself was in residence there. And definitely never at half-mast because even as one King or Queen dies, another immediately takes their place.

But much of the public was unsatisfied with this response, arguing the death of Diana was an exceptional circumstance that couldn't be ignored.

Stung somewhat by the criticism, the Queen gave in to a compromise. The Union Flag was flown at half mast as she left for Westminster Abbey on the day of

the funeral. Since this day, it has set a new precedent whereby whenever the Queen is not in residence at Buckingham Palace, the Union Flag flies overhead.

The controversy over the Royal Family's reaction to Diana's death subsided when the Queen spoke to the nation via a television broadcast on the day before the funeral service. In a candid fashion, Elizabeth II admitted it had been a difficult week for the family, as she had tried to shield her grandsons and allow them to mourn privately. She paid tribute to Diana and the work she had done around the world aiding various causes.

"We have all been trying in our different ways to cope. It is not easy to express a sense of loss, since the initial shock is often succeeded by a mixture of other feelings: disbelief, incomprehension, anger - and concern for those who remain. We have all felt those emotions in these last few days. So what I say to you now, as your Queen and as a grandmother, I say from my heart.

"First, I want to pay tribute to Diana myself. She was an exceptional and gifted human being. In good times and bad, she never lost her capacity to smile and laugh, nor to inspire others with her warmth and kindness. I admired and respected her - for her energy and commitment to others, and especially for her devotion to her two boys. This week at Balmoral, we have all been trying to help William and Harry come to terms with the devastating loss that they and the rest of us have suffered.

"No-one who knew Diana will ever forget her. Millions of others who never met her, but felt they knew her, will remember her. I for one believe there are lessons to be drawn from her life and from the extraordinary and moving reaction to her death. I share in your determination to cherish her memory."

Prince Charles, Prince Harry, Earl Spencer, Prince William and the Duke of Edinburgh at the funeral of Diana, September 6, 1997

2002

DEATH OF PRINCESS MARGARET

The Queen's younger sister experienced a great deal of illness and disability in her final years. Having started smoking at age 15, and remaining a heavy one throughout her life, she had to have part of her left lung removed in 1985.

In January 1993, Margaret was admitted to hospital for pneumonia, and in 1998 she suffered a mild stroke at her holiday home on the private island of Mustique in the West Indies.

The next year, she sustained serious scalding burns to her feet in a bathroom accident. This affected her mobility and meant she needed support to walk and even had to use a wheelchair at times.

And in January and March 2001, Princess Margaret suffered another series of strokes, leaving her partially blind and paralysed on the left side of her body.

Her final public appearances came at the 101st birthday celebrations of her mother, Elizabeth, as well as the 100th birthday celebrations for her aunt Princess Alice the Duchess of Gloucester.

On 9 February 2002, Princess Margaret suffered another stroke and died. She was 71 years old.

Her funeral followed just under a week later, on 15 February. The day was made all the more sombre as it was the 50th anniversary of her own father's funeral, King George VI.

As per her wishes, the ceremony was a private one, with just family and friends attending.

She chose to be cremated, something not normally done for members of the royal family. Her ashes were placed in the tomb of her parents.

To allow the public to commemorate her life, a state memorial service was held on 19 April.

DEATH OF ELIZABETH THE QUEEN MOTHER

Over the Christmas period of 2001, Elizabeth the Queen Mother, suffered from a persistent cold. At 101 years of age, this had the potential to turn quite serious, and so she was confined to the bedroom at her residence in Sandringham over those winter months.

Her final public engagement came on 22 November 2002 when she attended the recommissioning of HMS Ark Royal.

Despite her illness, she was determined to stay strong, at least in the public eye. When faced with the enormous tragedy of Princess Margaret's death on 9 February 2002, Elizabeth was determined to attend the funeral of her daughter.

Despite suffering a fall in her sitting room at Sandringham on 13 February, she travelled to Windsor by helicopter the next day. This came despite the huge concern from Queen Elizabeth II

who was worried what the stress of the journey would do to her ailing mother.

Princess Margaret's funeral was held on 15 February. Her mother arrived at the service in a people-carrier with blacked out windows. As per her wishes, she was shielded from the press so that no photographs of her in her wheelchair were taken. After the service, she returned to the Royal Lodge.

On 5 March, Elizabeth attended the luncheon of the annual lawn party of the Eton Beagles. She also watched the Cheltenham Races on television.

However from that point onwards, her health began to deteriorate. She became so frail that the decision was taken for her to finally exit from public life and be allowed to spend her finals days at the Royal Lodge.

On 30 March 2002, Elizabeth the Queen Mother, died. She had lived to the grand old age of 101. Her surviving daughter, Queen Elizabeth II, was at her bedside as she passed away.

In the following days, Elizabeth's body lay at the altar of the Royal Chapel of All Saints near the Royal Lodge, before being taken to London to be laid in state and for the funeral.

The funeral service began on 9 April 2002 at 9.48am in London, with the tenor bell at Westminster Abbey sounding 101 times.

The coffin was carried from the palace on a gun carriage. It started at Westminster Hall at 11.18am, with the coffin draped in Elizabeth's personal standard. Her crown rested on a cushion.

The journey was just three hundred metres, and it was accompanied by a large pipe band of 128 musicians drawn from 13 British and Commonwealth regiments.

Also joining the procession were the following Royal Family members: Prince Philip, Prince Charles, Prince Andrew, Princess Anne, Prince Edward, Prince William, Prince Harry, Viscount Linley, Peter Phillips, Daniel Chatto, The Duke of Gloucester, The Duke of Kent, Prince Michael of Kent and Timothy Laurence.

Also accompanying the royals were members of the Bowes-Lyon family as well as some of the Queen Mother's senior household staff.

At Westminster Abbey, the Royal Family were received by the Dean of Westminster Wesley Carr.

Following the service, Queen Elizabeth II and the Duke of Edinburgh then left the abbey by car and headed back towards Buckingham Palace, with a lunch for dignitaries held at 1.00pm.

Top: Queen Elizabeth, the Queen Mother, celebrates her 97th birthday at Clarence House, August 4, 1997

Bottom: The coffin of Queen Elizabeth the Queen Mother is carried away from Westminster Abbey following her funeral service

Main pic: Smiling at the warmth of her welcome, Queen Elizabeth II continuing her tour of the UK in celebration of her Golden Jubilee

Inset: Queen Elizabeth II with Prince Philip in the Gold State Coach during the procession from Buckingham Palace to St. Pauls, June 4, 2002

GOLDEN JUBILEE

The tragic events in the first few months of 2002, with the deaths of both Princess Margaret and Elizabeth the Queen Mother, put a dampener on the public mood heading into the middle of the year.

However the United Kingdom was still determined to give Queen Elizabeth II something to smile about, and so attention turned to the celebrations planned for her Golden Jubilee. This year marked 50 years since becoming Queen. This was something just five royals had achieved before her: Queen Victoria, George III, James VI and I of Scotland and England, Henry III and Edward III.

And celebrate they did.

On 4 June, one million people lined The Mall in London to watch a parade as well as an air force fly-past.

Prime Minister Tony Blair hosted a lavish dinner at 10 Downing Street.

And the Queen herself gave a special speech to both houses of the British Parliament at Westminster Hall. This was just the fifth time in her 50 year reign that the Queen had spoken to parliament entirely of her own volition (by convention, she does also read 'The Queen's Speech' annually to mark the traditional opening of the parliamentary year).

She spoke of those five decades as "unforgettable years", and remarked upon the changes to British life and society over that time. She admitted that the monarchy had to change as well to adapt to a changing country.

Prince Charles and The Duchess Of Cornwall,
Camilla Parker Bowles pose in the white drawing room
for the Official Wedding group photo following their
earlier marriage at The Guildhall, at Windsor Castle,
April 9, 2005

PRINCE CHARLES MARRIES CAMILLA

Prince Charles' second marriage, to Camilla Parker Bowles, took place on 9 April 2005.

Mindful of the history between the two, the media had coined the phrase "a wedding for grown-ups" to describe this occasion.

Prince Charles' relationship with Camilla had been long and controversial. She was often cast as the "other woman" in the public's mind during the tumultuous years Charles was married to Princess Diana.

Charles and Camilla first met in the middle of 1971. They were formally introduced by a mutual friend, and became close friends, eventually dating for a time.

The relationship took a more serious turn and Charles soon introduced her to members of his family. However in 1973 Charles left to tour with the Royal Navy overseas and things were put on hold. And shortly afterwards, the relationship broke down. A range of reasons have been offered by outside observers over the years as to what exactly happened. Some have suggested interference from Lord Mountbatten, disapproval from Elizabeth, The Queen Mother, or that Camilla had started to turn her attention to Andrew Parker Bowles, who she would later marry.

The assassination of Lord Mountbatten by members of the IRA in 1979 struck Prince Charles particularly hard. He had become something of a mentor to the Prince as he grew up, offering advice on everything from his royal duties to how to find a suitable woman to marry. It was during this time that the relationship between Charles and Camilla rekindled.

However Prince Charles would soon also establish a relationship with Diana Spencer. He fell in love and married her in 1980.

Nevertheless, speculation continued throughout the 1980s as to exactly how close Prince Charles remained with Camilla. It wasn't until 1992 that the rumours were confirmed when intimate telephone conversations were recorded and the transcripts published in the press.

Prince Charles and Princess Diana announced their separation in 1992, and their divorce became final in 1995. Meanwhile Camilla and Andrew Parker-Bowles also announced their divorce in 1995.

Mindful of the negative press surrounding their relationship, as well as the death of Diana, Charles and Camilla kept their appearances together out of the public eye throughout the late 90s. It wasn't until 1999 that she made a public appearance alongside the Prince at the Ritz Hotel in London, where they attended a birthday party in full view of the press.

Her first official meeting with the Queen, as Charles' partner, came in 2001, at the 60th birthday of King Constantine of Greece. This meeting was widely seen as the Queen giving her approval to the couple's relationship.

Main pic: The Prince of Wales, Prince Charles, and The Duchess of Cornwall, Camilla Parker-Bowles, on walkabout after the Service of Prayer and Dedication blessing their marriage

Inset: Prince Charles and Mrs Camilla Parker-Bowles depart Windsor Castle together by car to attend their Civil Ceremony

The rehabilitation was complete by 2005, when Clarence House announced Charles and Camilla were to marry. Polls showed a majority of people in the United Kingdom supported their marriage.

That's not to say the prospect of marriage was without controversy. After all, both Charles and Camilla were divorcees. And the Church of England still maintained rules surrounding re-marriage.

But it was now the 21st century. There was no serious objection offered by members of the Anglican clergy, or for that matter, any members of the British government.

This came in marked contrast to the events of the 1930s when King Edward VIII wanted to marry Wallis Simpson, and in the 1950s when Princess Margaret wanted to marry Peter Townsend. Society had evolved enough for divorce to be an accepted part of life, and for there to be no issue with a future King being himself divorced (even though he would become the head of the Anglican Church).

The Privy Council still had to meet to give effect to the Queen's approval of the marriage, which they duly did on 2 March 2005.

The Archbishop of Canterbury even put out a statement, "These arrangements have my strong support and are consistent with Church of England guidelines concerning remarriage which the Prince of Wales fully accepts as a committed Anglican and as prospective Supreme Governor of the Church of England".

The wedding was a civil ceremony at Windsor Guildhall on 9 April 2005.

It had actually been delayed for 24 hours. The original plan, announced upon the couple's engagement, had been for Charles and Camilla to marry on 8 April 2005. However the death of Pope John Paul II forced some late changes, with a number of guests (including Prince Charles' himself) having to attend the Pope's funeral service at the Vatican on that original date. Therefore, to give the guests enough time to attend both, Charles and Camilla decided to push everything back.

There were actually two services. The first conducted in the presence of the couple's families (although The Queen did not attend), and the second was a Church of England blessing held at St George's Chapel (this the Queen did attend). Television cameras did not broadcast the wedding service to the public, however they were there for the blessing and viewers watched on the BBC.

For the wedding service, Camilla wore a cream coloured dress and coat with a wide brimmed cream coloured hat. For the blessing afterward, she wore a floor-length embroidered pale blue and gold coat over a matching chiffon gown and dramatic spray of golden feathers in her hair.

There was no official 'best man' or 'maid of honour' (or 'supporters' as the royals prefer to call those roles) at this wedding. Instead, Prince William and Tom Bowles acted as witnesses to the ceremony, presented the rings to their parents, and signed the register.

The Queen and Prince Philip would later host a reception for the newly married couple at Windsor Castle.

TRH Prince Charles, The Prince of Wales and The Duchess of Cornwall, Camilla Parker-Bowles pose for the Official Wedding photograph with their children and parents (L-R Prince Harry, Prince William, Laura and Tom Parker-Bowles Front: Queen Elizabeth II, Prince Philip, Bruce Shand), in the White Drawing Room at Windsor Castle

Queen Elizabeth II sits in the Regency Room at Buckingham Palace, as she looks at some of the cards which have been sent to her for her 80th birthday, April 20, 2006

THE QUEEN TURNS 80

Queen Elizabeth turned 80 years old on 21 April 2006.

Her preference is always to celebrate her actual birthday privately, amongst her family and friends. This leaves the more public celebrations until later in the year when the official Queen's Birthday holiday is observed across the country.

Even so, this special occasion was marked publicly with gun salutes in central London at midday. There was a 41 gun salute in Hyde Park, a 21 gun salute in Windsor Great Park and a 62 gun salute from the Tower of London.

One of the first public displays to mark the day was the raising of a huge Royal Standard – used for celebrations such as this one. Measuring 38 feet long and 19 feet wide, it was raised over the Round Tower, the highest point of Windsor Castle, where the Queen had started her day.

The Queen met thousands of well-wishers as she embarked on an informal walkabout around the town of Windsor.

Buckingham Palace had announced the Queen had received as many as 20,000 cards and 17,000 emails – sent via a special website created to mark Her Majesty's 80th birthday.

From Prime Minister Tony Blair and members of the UK Government, she received a china tea set made by Spode pottery in Staffordshire.

Blair's official spokesman said the gift was something Buckingham Palace had indicated the Queen would like.

Meanwhile, a special birthday message came from members aboard a Royal Navy aircraft carrier, who lined up in formation to spell out "HAPPY 80th".

The Queen thanked all birthday well-wishers in a statement, saying "I would like to thank the many thousands of people from this country and overseas who have sent me cards and messages on my 80th birthday. I have been very touched by what you have written and would like to express my gratitude to you all".

Dressed in a vibrant pink coat and hat, Elizabeth accepted gifts, cards and flowers as she and husband Prince Philip walked around Windsor for about 45 minutes.

Well-wishers had arrived in Windsor much earlier in the day, hoping to catch a glimpse of the birthday lady and perhaps even personally offer their birthday congratulations if she got close enough. As many as 20,000 people were estimated to be there, including Jennifer Hawkins of Worthing, West Sussex who told the BBC, "I just wanted to be involved and wish the Queen a Happy Birthday. She works so extremely hard and just presents herself so magnificently".

Seventeen year old Chris Foskett admitted, "None of my friends would come with me but I think she is great looking for her age, isn't she? She keeps the country together. You need somebody to represent your country. Politicians can't do it".

Later in the day, her son Prince Charles delivered a special birthday tribute on BBC Radio 4.

"Now I find it hard to believe my own mother, the Queen, is today celebrating her 80th birthday.

"And it gives me enormous pride to be able to congratulate her publicly in this way.

"It's hard to believe that my grandfather, King George VI, was the same age as I am now when he died, and that my mother succeeded him when so young – the same age, in fact, as my sons are now.

"Now that there is no doubt that the world in which my mother grew up, and indeed the world in which she first became Queen, has changed beyond all recognition.

"But during this, she has shown the most remarkable steadfastness and fortitude, always remaining a figure of reassuring calm and dependability, an example to so many of service, duty and devotion in a world of sometimes bewildering change and disorientation.

"For nearly 60 of 80 years, she has been my darling Mama, and my sentiments today are those of a proud and loving son who hopes that you will join with me in wishing the Queen the happiest of happy birthdays, together with the fervent prayer that there will be countless memorable returns of the day."

In the evening, the birthday celebrations took place at Kew Palace, a royal palace located on the banks of the River Thames west of the London city.

A restoration of the historic building had recently been completed and Prince Charles arranged to host a private party to celebrate his mother's special day. This would be the first time since King George III stayed at the palace in private that a monarch had dined there. A gap of some two hundred years.

On the evening of 21 April, some 26 close members of the Royal Family, along with a crowd of two hundred well-wishers stood outside the palace and enjoyed a spectacular fireworks display over Kew Gardens.

Then the party went inside where the Royal Family gathered in a small dining room to enjoy a meal together. The menu included simple English food – Hebridean smoked salmon, Juniper roast loin of Sandringham estate venison and a chocolate sponge cake filled with a Highgrove fruit filling.

On 6 December, the Queen attended another birthday celebration to mark her 80th year.

The party had been organised by her cousin, Lady Elizabeth Anson, and was held at the Ritz Hotel in London.

Dressed in an ankle length blue sparkling dress, the Queen arrived alongside husband Prince Philip. She paused briefly on the steps to wave at a small crowd of well-wishers before going inside to meet the guests.

Those who were there included the Earl and Countess of Wessex, Princesses Beatrice and Eugenie, the Duke and Duchess of Gloucester, Princess Alexandra and Peter Philips, and even former King Constantine of Greece, who lives in exile in London.

The attendees stayed tight-lipped about what went on at the party, insisting this was a "completely private" event designed to celebrate the end of a special year for the Queen.

Main pic: Queen Elizabeth II is taking part in her traditional walk in the town to celebrate her 80th Birthday, April 21, 2006

Inset top: Queen Elizabeth II stands with Prince Charles, Prince of Wales, to watch a firework display at Kew Palace

Inset bottom: Queen Elizabeth II and Prince Philip, Duke of Edinburgh arrive at St Paul's Cathedral for a service of thanksgiving held in honour of the Queen's 80th birthday, June 15, 2006

PRINCE WILLIAM MARRIES KATE MIDDLETON

Prince William met Kate when they were students at the University of St Andrews. They both lived at St Salvator's Hall during their first year, and later shared accommodation in the town.

Kate, or Catherine Middleton, is the eldest of three children born to Michael and Carole Middleton. She went to St Andrew's School in Pangbourne, Marlborough College, as well as the University of St Andrews. After graduating she worked in retail, as well as at her parents' business as an accessories buyer/catalogue photographer.

The couple began dating in 2003 and their relationship became the subject of intense media scrutiny. As a direct heir to the British throne, the women in Prince William's life were always bound to come under the media glare. However both Prince William and Kate felt the intrusion became too restricting, and made several complaints over the years they dated.

Parallels were drawn between the intense interest in Princess Diana's life and the role the paparazzi played at the end of her life. There were fears the constant press intrusion would push Kate away, and give her second thoughts about spending her life within the constant glare of royal family life.

It came to a head in April 2007, when the couple split up, although no official reason was ever given for why Prince William and Kate ended the relationship. In any case the separation was short-lived. Within a few months royal watchers soon noticed Kate was back in Prince William's life. And by the end of the year they had rekindled their romance.

In October 2010, Prince William proposed to Kate in Kenya during a 10 day trip to the Lewa Wildlife Conservancy. The engagement became public knowledge a month later. It was revealed that Prince William had used the same engagement ring that had belonged to his mother, Princess Diana.

On 29 April 2011, the Queen's eldest grandchild, Prince William, married Kate Middleton. The day had been declared a public holiday throughout the United Kingdom. As many as 5,000 street parties were held across the country, and the crowds lining the wedding procession route through the streets of London were numbered around one million people.

That route went between Buckingham Palace and Westminster Abbey via The Mall, passing Clarence House, by Horse Guards Road, Horse Guards Parade, through Horse Guards Arch, the South Side of Parliament Square and Broad Sanctuary.

The cost of the wedding was taken care of by the Royal Family and the Middletons, while security and transport were covered by the Treasury. Prince William and Kate asked the public that any donations be made to charities in place of the

Prince William exchanges rings with his bride Catherine Middleton in front of the Archbishop of Canterbury, Rowan Williams inside Westminster Abbey, April 29, 2011

Main pic: Prince William and Kate Middleton pose for photographs after their engagement announcement in the State Apartments of St James Palace, November 16, 2010

Inset left: Their Royal Highnesses Prince William, Duke of Cambridge and Catherine, Duchess of Cambridge journey by carriage procession to Buckingham Palace following their marriage at Westminster Abbey, April 29, 2011

Inset right: Kate Middleton and Prince William on the day of their graduation ceremony at St Andrew's University, June 23, 2005

traditional wedding gifts. They set up The Prince William and Catherine Middleton Charitable Gift Fund, which raised money for the Christchurch Earthquake Appeal, the Royal Flying Doctor Service, and the Zoological Society of London, among other causes.

The Dean of Westminster, John Hall, presided over the service. Archbishop of Canterbury, Rowan Williams, conducted the marriage, with Richard Chartress, the Bishop of London, preaching the sermon; while a reading was given by the bride's brother James.

Kate's bridal dress had been designed by Sarah Burton, a London based designer at Alexander McQueen. It was made of satin and featured an overlaid lace bodice and appliquéd skirt. Her veil was held in place by a Cartier Scroll Tiara, which had been lent to her by the Queen.

That dazzling piece of headgear had originally been commissioned in 1936. Prince Albert (later to become King George VI) gave it to his wife Elizabeth (later the Queen Mother). In 1946, she passed it on to her daughter, Princess Elizabeth, for her 18th birthday.

The wedding service started with a procession, featuring The Queen, Prince Philip and members of the clergy. Shortly afterwards, Kate walked down the aisle her proud father beside her. Her maid of honour, sister Pippa Middleton, and junior attendances followed.

As she made the three and a half minute journey from one end to the other, the choir sang an anthem by Sir Hubert Parry.

In the marriage vows, Prince William and Kate promised to "love, comfort, honour and keep" each other. This was then sealed by the exchange of a single ring.

In his sermon, the bishop urged the couple to live selflessly, each remembering the needs of each other and seeking to transform each other by love, rather than seeking to reform.

Upon leaving Westminster Abbey, the bells of the church pealed, and Prince William and Kate passed through a guard of individually selected men and women from various services. The crowds outside greeted them with huge cheers.

It was also on this day that the press began to refer to Kate as Catherine, her proper name. The Queen also bestowed upon her and her new husband the new titles the Duke and Duchess of Cambridge.

The bridal couple departed the Abbey precinct in a 1902 State Landau drawn by four white horses with postilions and attendant footmen and guarded by a mounted escort of the Life Guard.

The Queen, alongside other members of the Royal Family, followed in coaches drawn by the Queen's Cleveland Bay horses as well as in state cars.

At 1.25pm, the newly married couple appeared on the balcony of Buckingham Palace to watch an aerial flypast.

The wedding service guest list comprised over 1,900 people inside Westminster Abbey. A reception hosted by The Queen attracted 600 guests, while 300 people had the privilege of going to an evening dinner hosted by Prince Charles.

At the evening reception, singer Ellie Goulding performed a version of Elton John's "Your Song" for the couple's first dance.

The event ended with a small fireworks display from the palace grounds.

DIAMOND JUBILEE

Only Queen Victoria in 1897 had reached 60 years as British sovereign, before Queen Elizabeth also celebrated her Diamond Jubilee in 2012.

On 18 May, the Queen hosted an informal lunch at Windsor Castle for more than twenty current or former monarchs from other countries.

On 3 June, the River Thames was full of special boats – some 670 to be precise. A parade had been organised by the Thames Diamond Jubilee Foundation. It took a route from Wandsworth, out in the south-west, to the Tower of London.

The procession of boats was approximately 7.5 miles long, and was separated into sections.

Among the flotillas were boats carrying The Royal Jubilee Bells, gondolas, Dunkirk Little Ships, a boat carrying the London Philharmonic Orchestra, and various historic vessels.

The Queen and Prince Philip sailed on board the royal barge MV *Spirit of Chartwell*. It had been decorated with thousands of flowers and plants, and featured drapery with the arms of Commonwealth countries. Also on board were Prince Charles, Prince William, Catherine the Duchess of Cambridge, and Prince Harry.

Upon completion of the river journey, as the *Spirit of Chartwell* approached Tower Bridge, the Queen was saluted by the guns, the naval cadets and veterans aboard HMS *Belfast*.

As the barge docked, it was expected the Queen would watch the rest of the procession inside. However, despite wet weather, the Queen chose to remain aboard The *Spirit of Chartwell*. She remained for nearly four hours, waving and acknowledging spectators.

On 4 June, the lighting of beacons took place. This had become something of a tradition to mark the Queen's anniversaries. Originally, organisers had planned to set the number of beacons to be lit at 2,012, however by the closing date of registration they had upwards of 4,000 beacons submitted in the United Kingdom alone.

The first beacon was lit on the grounds of Apifo'ou College in Nuku'alofa, Tonga. Other nations involved included Kenya, Australia, New Zealand, India, the Seychelles, Sri Lanka and several nations in the Caribbean.

In the United Kingdom, the Queen helped to ignite the first beacon outside Buckingham Palace at 10.30pm, and the lightings proceeded across the country before ending across the Atlantic in Canada some eight hours later.

Unfortunately the celebrations were tempered somewhat by a serious illness for Prince Philip. Just about to turn 91 years old, the Duke had been hospitalised with a bladder infection on 4 June. Doctors ordered him to rest and recover, and he was unable to attend many of the official events planned over the course of the Golden Jubilee celebrations.

*Queen Elizabeth II waves from the royal barge
'Spirit of Chartwell' as it sails past the Houses of
Parliament during the Thames Diamond Jubilee
Pageant on the River Thames June 3, 2012*

In a speech delivered at the conclusion of the Diamond Jubilee Concert, Prince Charles told the audience how sad he was for his father not to be there that night. He urged them to cheer as loud as they could so Prince Philip could hear them in hospital.

The Diamond Jubilee celebrations were also notable for what took place around the world, in the various nations of the Commonwealth.

In Australia, Prince Charles and the Duchess of Cornwall toured in November. They participated in various community led events designed to recognise the reign of Prince Charles' mother.

Following their tour of Australia, Prince Charles and Camilla arrived across the Tasman Sea in New Zealand. They visited Auckland, Wellington, Christchurch and Manawatu.

Prince Harry toured The Bahamas, including attending a reception for youth leaders and meeting the Governor-General.

Canada celebrated Diamond Jubilee Week in February. The Peace Tower, standing as the focal point of the Canadian Houses of Parliament in Ottawa, played a tribute to Elizabeth II, while the monarch's personal standard was unfurled on Parliament Hill. Some 60,000 Canadian Queen Elizabeth II Diamond Jubilee Medals were distributed to citizens and to permanent residents. Prince Charles and the Duchess of Cornwall toured the country in May, making stops in New Brunswick, Ontario and Saskatchewan.

Main pic: The manpowered section of boats passes the London Eye and The Houses of Parliament during the Queen's Thames Diamond Jubilee River Pageant

Inset top: Queen Elizabeth II waves to the crowd during the Queen's Thames Diamond Jubilee River Pageant

Inset second from top: Guardsmen line the stage at the start of the Queen's Diamond Jubilee Concert at Buckingham Palace

Inset third from top: The Diamond Jubilee Beacon being lit on top of Otley Chevin, West Yorkshire

Inset bottom: In Australia on the second leg of a Diamond Jubilee Tour, Prince Charles, Prince of Wales and Camilla, Duchess of Cornwall taste wine at the Penfolds Magill State Winery Adelaide, November 7, 2012

Prince William, Duke of Cambridge and Catherine, Duchess of Cambridge, depart The Lindo Wing with their newborn son Prince George of Cambridge at St Mary's Hospital, July 23, 2013

THE BIRTH OF PRINCE GEORGE

Almost as soon as Prince William and Catherine had married, speculation started as to when the Duchess of Cambridge would be expecting a child. It took less than a year, with Buckingham Palace announcing on 3 December 2012 that Catherine was pregnant.

This announcement did come sooner than the royal family would have liked. The Duchess was just twelve weeks into the pregnancy, but because of her being admitted to hospital with acute morning sickness, an announcement needed to be made to head off the inevitable barrage of rumours.

On 22 July 2013, the Duchess was admitted to St Mary's Hospital in London in the early stages of labour.

After a labour period lasting ten-and-a-half hours, she gave birth to a boy weighing 8lbs 6oz, in the Lindo Wing, the very same location where both Prince William and Prince Harry had been born. The time of birth was recorded as 4.24pm.

The customary formal bulletin announcing the royal birth was displayed on an easel outside Buckingham Palace, although in a break with tradition the news was first conveyed in a press release from palace officials.

TV cameras outside the hospital captured a man dressed in a town crier outfit ringing his bell. Shouting "Oh yea, Oh yea" he informed viewers that "The Duchess of Cambridge was safely delivered of a son". He had no links to Buckingham Palace but was merely an ordinary citizen wanting to add a touch of history and ceremony to this important news.

The Duchess would feel well enough to leave hospital the next day with the newborn. The Duchess appeared outside the hospital, alongside Prince William, cradling her new child in her arms. The crowds of people who had waited patiently to see them clapped and cheered, while the couple stopped and posed for photographs in front of a sea of cameras.

Prince William joked, "He's got her looks, thankfully", to which Catherine replied 'No, no, I'm not sure about that".

But Prince William continued, saying his son has already got "more hair than me, thank God".

On the following day the baby boy's name was announced as George Alexander Louis.

The Queen had already been informed of the choice of name before the announcement had been made. George was the name her father took upon becoming King in 1936, and was also the name of her grandfather, King George V, who reigned from 1910 to 1936. In total there have been six King Georges, and there may well be a seventh before this new George ever becomes King. Prince Charles has said he may take the name King George VII upon succession, so as not to associate himself with the name King Charles (which has not had a good run in British history).

Alexander was a favoured name of Catherine's, while the name Louis is a reference to Lord Louis Mountbatten.

The announcement of the names had actually come relatively quickly compared to previous royal births. In 1982, it took the world seven days to find out the name of Prince William, while in 1948 it took a whole month for Prince Charles to be officially named. But the changing nature of technology and communication meant that in the 21st century, the name of such an important child could never be kept quiet for long.

On the Tuesday evening following the birth, the Queen attended a reception at Buckingham Palace and says she was "thrilled" to have another great-grandchild. This was her third. One of Princess Anne's children, Peter Phillips has two daughters with his wife Autumn Phillips – Savannah Ann Kathleen Phillips (born in 2010) and Isla Elizabeth Phillips (born earlier in 2012).

The following day, the Queen spent 30 minutes with Prince George. This particular birth would mark just the second time in royal history that three generations of direct heirs to the British throne had been alive at the same time. With Queen Elizabeth II as sovereign, there was Prince Charles, Prince William and now Prince George. The only other time this had been possible was during the final years of the Queen Victoria's reign.

After a short stay at Kensington Palace, the new mum, dad and child went to the Middleton family home in the Berkshire village of Bucklebury. Prince William had taken two weeks of paternity leave as the couple adjusted to their new roles.

On Friday 2 August, the birth was officially registered. Photographs of the birth certificate were released to the media, with the child's name officially known as His Royal Highness Prince George Alexander Louis of Cambridge.

Main pic: Prince William, Duke of Cambridge, Catherine, Duchess of Cambridge and Prince George of Cambridge meet a Bilby called George as they visit Taronga Zoo (Sydney Australia), April 20, 2014 in Sydney, Australia

Inset top: Catherine, Duchess of Cambridge carries her son Prince George of Cambridge after his christening at the Chapel Royal in St James's Palace, October 23, 2013

Inset bottom: Queen Elizabeth II, Prince William, Duke of Cambridge, Prince George of Cambridge, Catherine, Duchess of Cambridge and Prince Phillip, Duke of Edinburgh, during the annual Trooping The Colour ceremony at Buckingham Palace, June 13, 2015

MEETING U.S. PRESIDENTS

Queen Elizabeth II has met 12 Presidents of the United States of America.

The first meeting, President Harry Truman, came before she succeeded the British throne. As Princess Elizabeth, she met him on 2 November 1951.

Her first state visit to America as Queen came in 1957. She attended a State Banquet on 20 October as an official guest of President Dwight D. Eisenhower.

There was intense media interest in June 1961 when President John F. Kennedy dined at Buckingham Palace, alongside wife Jacqueline. 'JFK's' celebrity status had travelled across the Atlantic, and the British were keen to see this 'younger' president alongside the Queen.

The only President the Queen never met is President Lyndon B. Johnson. She was unable to attend the funeral of President Kennedy after his assassination, as she was pregnant with Prince Edward at the time. And no subsequent opportunities came up for either leader to meet the other during Johnson's time in office.

In February 1969, President Richard Nixon travelled to the United Kingdom and had lunch with the Queen at Buckingham Palace.

The Queen met President Gerald Ford in July 1976 with photographers happy to capture images of her and the President dancing. She had travelled to the White House to take part in the United States' bicentennial celebrations.

In May 1977, President Jimmy Carter travelled to London. He was there for an economic summit and also accepted the Queen's invitation to Buckingham Palace. Somewhat controversially, President Carter made a bit of a faux pas when he broke protocol and kissed the Queen Mother on the lips as he greeted her. This did not go down well with the Queen Mother who later remarked it was the first time a man had done that since her husband King George VI had died.

President Ronald Reagan stayed at Windsor Castle along with his wife Nancy in June 1982. The former movie star joining the Queen for a horse ride.

The Queen would make a return visit to the United States in 1983 and again met President Reagan.

In May 1991, the Queen yet again returned to the United States and met President George H W Bush. He would meet her at the White House before she flew to Baltimore to watch her very first game of Major League Baseball.

She met President Bill Clinton on several occasions, including in June 1994 when the pair attended a banquet held for the 50th anniversary of the D-Day landings in Normandy, France. President Clinton also travelled to the United Kingdom in 2000 and joined the Queen for tea at Buckingham Palace.

A funny moment came in May 2007 when the Queen was guest of honour at the White House with President George W Bush. The notoriously gaffe-prone President had made a verbal slip up when he mentioned the Queen had helped the United States celebrate the bicentennial in 1776 (rather than 1976). As he realised his error he winked at the Queen, and turned back to the audience and admitted sheepishly "She gave me a look that only a mother could give a child".

In April 2009, President Barack Obama travelled to the United Kingdom for a G20 summit. He took the opportunity to meet the Queen and Prince Philip at Buckingham Palace. Alongside wife Michelle Obama, the President gave the Queen a gift – a personalised iPod containing a video of her visit in 2007. In return the Queen presented the President and First Lady with a silver-framed signed photograph of herself and Prince Philip.

Beyond 2016, the Queen has the opportunity to meet a 13th President of the United States. Although given the Queen's advancing age it is likely that the next President will have to make his or her way to the United Kingdom for that historic occasion.

Main pic (opposite page): Queen Elizabeth II speaks with US President Barack Obama during a group photo of world leaders attending the D-Day 70th Anniversary ceremonies at Chateau de Benouville, France, June 6, 2014

Left: Princess Elizabeth talking with President Harry S. Truman, Washington DC, November 1951

Second from left: US President Gerald Ford, dancing with Queen Elizabeth II at the ball at the White House, Washington, 1976

Second from right: Queen Elizabeth II presents US President Ronald Reagan with an honorary Knighthood at Buckingham Palace, June 14, 1989

Right: Prior to a banquet in honour of the President of the United States, HRH Queen Elizabeth II (second right) with Prince Philip (far left) together with American President John F. Kennedy (far right) and his wife and First Lady Jacqueline, June 15, 1961

IRISH STATE VISIT

Michael D. Higgins' visit to the United Kingdom in April 2014 marked the first time a President of Ireland had made an official State Visit across the Irish Sea.

It came just three years after Queen Elizabeth II and Prince Philip had made a state visit to Ireland, also marking the first time that had happened as well.

President Higgins had departed Ireland on 7 April, and spent the first evening in the United Kingdom at the Kensington Hotel in South Kensington.

The formal State Visit got underway the following day and was scheduled to last for four days. Higgins and his wife Sabina met Prince Charles and Camilla, the Duchess of Cornwall at the Irish embassy. Together they travelled via royal limousine to Windsor.

It was there that the Queen formally welcomed President Higgins and his wife. Elizabeth II wore a coat of sky blue cashmere over a moss green and dove grey Paisley print dress. Her hat had been decorated with hand-made green feather flowers.

They all travelled together in royal limousines to the Royal Dais on Datchet Road in Windsor. The town had been decked out in both the British Union Flags as well as Irish Tricolours. Some people in the town admitted feeling a bit nervous about this visit and the potential for trouble, given the complicated history between the United Kingdom and Ireland.

The Queen and Prince Philip conducted a formal ceremony of welcome for their guests. The guests were honoured with two separate gun salutes before entering the castle in the Australian State Coach.

Later on, the royal party and visitors left in horse drawn carriages and made their way over to Windsor Castle. There, the President and Duke of Edinburgh inspected a Guard of Honour provided by the Queen's company Grenadier Guards.

President Higgins presented a ceremonial red coat to its regimental mascot, an Irish Wolfhound called Domhnall of Shantamon.

He also took the time to explore Windsor Castle, including taking in the Irish-related items on show at the Royal Collection there.

Afterwards, the British and Irish contingents left for London. They visited Westminster Abbey, where President Higgins laid a wreath at the Grave of the Unknown Warrior and paid his respects with a bow to the tomb of Louis, the Earl of Mountbatten, who had died in a 1979 IRA terrorist bombing.

The President then made his way across to the Palace of Westminster, where he addressed both houses of the UK Parliament.

He spoke of being graciously and warmly welcomed by Her Majesty the Queen, and remarked that the relationship between the two countries has achieved a closeness and warmth that once seemed unachievable.

*Queen Elizabeth II stands with President of Ireland
Michael D Higgins during a ceremonial welcome at
Windsor Castle, April 8, 2014*

"We acknowledge that past, but, even more, we wholeheartedly welcome the considerable achievement of today's reality – the mutual respect, friendship and cooperation which exists between our two countries."

That evening, Michael and Sabina Higgins were the guests of honour at a State Banquet hosted by the Queen at Windsor Castle. There were 160 guests in attendance, including a few celebrities like actors Daniel Day-Lewis and Dame Judi Dench, as well as rugby star Brian O'Driscoll.

Before the dinner, the Queen gave a speech. She remarked on the vast amount of time it had taken for the United Kingdom and Ireland to reach a point where a visit such as this was possible.

"The castle was founded by William the Conqueror almost a thousand years ago. And a thousand years ago this very month, across the Irish Sea, Brian Boru, the most celebrated of Ireland's High Kings, lost his life at the Battle of Clontarf. Yet, despite ten centuries of intervening history, Windsor Castle has had to wait until today to see a formal visit by a Head of State of Ireland.

"But even more pleasing, since then, is that we, the Irish and British, are becoming good and dependable neighbours and better friends, finally shedding our inhibitions about seeing the best in each other.

"Mr President, the goal of modern British-Irish relations can be simply stated. It is that we, who inhabit these islands, should live together as neighbours and friends. Respectful of each other's nationhood, sovereignty and traditions. Cooperation to our mutual benefit. At ease in each other's company."

President Higgins then offered a speech in reply, acknowledging the fraught relationship between the two countries.

"Ireland and Britain live in both the shadow and in the shelter of one another, and so it has been since the dawn of history. We celebrate what has been achieved but we must also constantly renew our commitment to a process that requires vigilance and care."

He proposed a toast to Her Majesty, and also praised her for making an historic visit to Dublin in 2011. He noted how that visit had paved the way for himself to visit the United Kingdom in a formal capacity three years later.

Higgins and his wife were then honoured as guests of the Queen at Windsor Castle for the remainder of their stay in the United Kingdom.

This banquet was also significant for another reason. One of the people invited was Northern Ireland Deputy First Minister and former IRA commander Martin McGuiness. This provoked a bit of criticism from those who still viewed McGuiness as a terrorist. A protest had been held outside the castle grounds in Windsor, with the sister of a person killed in an IRA bombing calling for the arrest of McGuiness. The Queen attempted to address this in her speech, "We will remember our past, but we shall no longer allow our past to ensnare our future".

Over the following days, President Higgins would visit a number of places. He and Prince Andrew, the Duke of York, went to the Grand Stairs at Windsor Castle to view the colours of the 1922 disbanded Irish Regiments. He attended a Northern Ireland themed reception hosted by the Queen. On the morning of the final day, the President and his wife farewelled the Queen and Prince Philip and thanked them for their hospitality.

Main pic and inset above: Guests listen during a speech by Queen Elizabeth II in honour of the President of Ireland Michael D. Higgins, April 8, 2014

Inset below: Members of the Irish Guard march past the British and the Irish flags during the state visit of Irish President Michael D Higgins

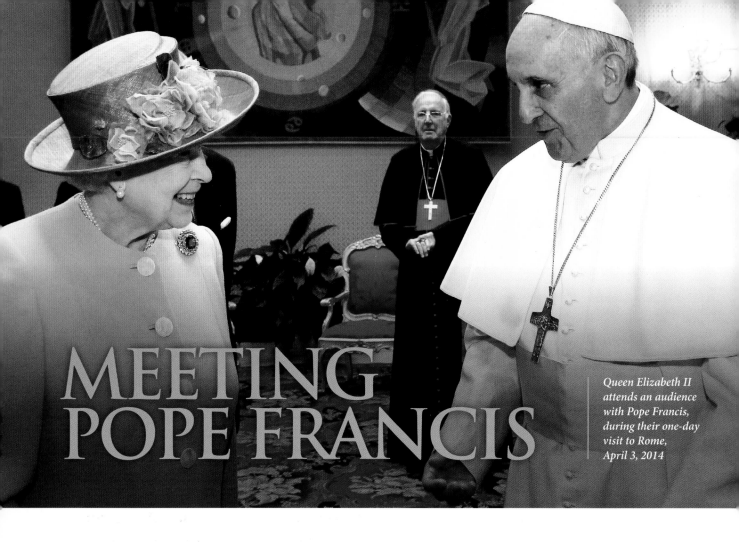

MEETING POPE FRANCIS

Queen Elizabeth II attends an audience with Pope Francis, during their one-day visit to Rome, April 3, 2014

The Queen and Prince Philip travelled to Rome in April 2014, her first journey overseas since a visit to Australia in 2011.

Originally, Buckingham Palace had been planning for the Queen to visit the new Pope some time in 2013. However she became ill that year, and it was decided that all international travel should be postponed for some months to allow her to rest and recover.

It was a clear sign that the Queen's age was going to have an impact on future travel plans. She had visited 116 countries over the past six decades of her reign, but would now be undertaking far less travel.

But the Pope is an important global figure, and now that she was ready, the Queen and Prince Philip flew out to Rome on 3 April. This would be her first visit to the Italian capital in 14 years.

The royal couple first met Italy's President Giorgio Napolitano and his wife Clio at the Quirinal Palace. President Napolitano has been a long-time friend of the Queen.

Afterwards, they travelled to the Vatican to meet Pope Francis. It had been a little over a year since Francis had been elected Pope, following the resignation of Pope Benedict XVI. This was the first time the Queen had met the new Pope. She had previously been received by Pope John XXIII in 1961, as well as Pope John Paul II in 1980 and again in 2000.

On this particular visit, the Queen wore a lilac coat over a lilac and green chiffon dress and matching lilac hat. This is instead of wearing black, which is considered the norm when meeting the pope. Buckingham Palace and the Vatican agreed to this to emphasise the friendly nature of the visit.

The Queen and Prince Philip arrived at the Vatican via a side gate, rather than using the front of St Peter's Square, where all the tourists were.

Upon meeting, the Queen apologised for running a bit behind schedule. "Sorry to keep you waiting. We were having a very pleasant lunch with the president."

The Queen presented Pope Francis with gifts. These were from her royal estates at Buckingham Palace, Windsor Castle, Sandringham Castle and Balmoral Castle. There were 18 items in total, including two types of honey, chutney, soap and 'Coronation Best Bitter' beer.

The Duke of Edinburgh held up a bottle of malt whiskey, and told the Pope "It's from Balmoral, up in Scotland".

A Vatican official later told the Press the Pope would probably share the food gifts with other residents of the guest house at the Vatican where he has resided since his election. Other gifts would be donated to the poor, in keeping with the Pope's message of compassion for those most marginalised in society.

In return, Pope Francis presented the Queen with an orb decorated with a silver cross, intended for Prince George, who at that point was just ten months old.

An orb is a traditional emblem of power for Christian monarchs. This one sat on a silver base, with the words "Pope Francis to His Royal Highness Prince George of Cambridge" transcribed in English.

"It's for the little boy" the Pope told the Queen in his native Spanish.

The Queen appreciated the gift, and told the Pope she was certain Prince George would be "thrilled by it", but added "when he is a little older".

Other gifts shared between the pair were signed royal photographs in silver frames, as well as a replica of a decree from the Vatican archives.

The Pope also had a gift for Prince Philip – a set of papal medallions in gold, silver and bronze. The 92 year old Prince thanked the Pope for the kind gift, and joked that "it's the only gold medal I've ever won!"

Following the brief introduction, the Pope, Queen and Duke of Edinburgh met privately for around 25 minutes.

In keeping with the more informal nature of the visit, they met in the Pope's study, rather than the more opulent Apostolic Palace that is more commonly used when receiving heads of state at the Vatican.

Both the Vatican and Buckingham Palace favoured this more relaxed meeting. There were also concerns about the distance and stairs the elderly Queen would've had to negotiate had she met the Pope in the Apostolic Palace.

The whole meeting was largely viewed as part of a long process aimed at improving relations between the two Christian churches– the Pope as head of the Roman Catholic Church, and the Queen as Supreme Governor of the Church of England. Though the relationship between Pope Francis and Justin Welby, the Archbishop of Canterbury is cordial, the Queen has been keen to improve understanding between the two Churches.

Observers couldn't help but wonder if the Queen and Pope would go over some rather controversial ground. The visit came roughly 32 years after the Falklands War, fought between the United Kingdom and Argentina. Pope Francis is Argentinian, and the lingering memories of that 1982 conflict still provokes bitter feelings among many of his fellow country folk.

To head off any controversy, Britain's ambassador to the Holy See, Nigel Baker, had actually addressed the issue on Vatican Radio beforehand. "The Vatican has been clear with us, including in the last week and at a very senior level, that their long-standing position of neutrality on this issue remains in force."

Instead, the theme of the meeting was to focus on the shared roots of the Christian Faith. Indeed, the meeting had come on the 100th anniversary of the re-establishing of diplomatic ties between the Vatican and the United Kingdom.

Later in the day the Queen and Prince Philip flew back to Britain, via Rome's Ciampino airport. The entire visit to Rome and the Vatican had lasted just five hours.

A VISIT TO FRANCE

French Prime Minister Manuel Valls (2nd L), Britain's Queen Elizabeth II (C) and her husband Prince Philip (L), Duke of Edinburgh, Britain's Prince Charles, Prince of Wales (2nd R) his wife Camilla, the Duchess of Cornwall, attend a bi-national France-UK D-Day commemoration ceremony at the British War Cemetery of Bayeux, June 6, 2014

Queen Elizabeth enjoyed a three-day state visit to France in June 2014.

The visit had been organised as part of the commemorations for the 70th anniversary of the D-Day landings at Normandy, a major turning point in the Second World War.

The Queen's first day in France saw her honouring France's war dead by laying a wreath at a national monument.

She and the Duke of Edinburgh had arrived in Paris via a Eurostar train. At Gare du Nord station, they were greeted by Britain's ambassador to France, Sir Peter Ricketts.

They were also warmly received by French President Francois Hollande. The Queen wore a pink fine summer wool outfit, as well as a Williamson brooch.

She joined President Hollande at the Tomb of the Unknown Soldier, located beneath the

Arc de Triomphe in Paris. The Queen left a floral tribute in memory to those soldiers who died unrecognised but still played a vital part in ensuring France's freedom.

Both the Queen and President bowed their heads in a mark of respect to all those who died in major conflicts. The national anthems of both France and the United Kingdom were played.

Afterwards, the Queen and President travelled the Champs Elysees, escorted by 146 mounted members of the Republican Guard.

The following day, the Queen and Duke of Edinburgh travelled to Normandy on the north-western coast. They visited the beaches where some 70 years ago, allied forces began their invasion which would ultimately end in the liberation of France and help contribute to the eventual defeat of Nazi Germany. They were joined by Prince Charles, Camilla the Duchess of Cornwall, Prince William, and Catherine the Duchess of Cambridge.

Other world leaders present in Normandy included United Kingdom Prime Minister David Cameron, United States President Barack Obama, Australian Prime Minister Tony Abbott, Canadian Prime Minister Stephen Harper and Russian President Vladimir Putin.

Even German chancellor Angela Merkel was there, symbolising the friendship between the European countries, now that the war was 70 years in the past.

French President Francois Hollande told those in attendance at Sword Beach that the world leaders owed it to those who sacrificed their lives on D-Day to build a "fairer world". He also called on ordinary people to show the same courage in fighting threats to peace as the soldiers did on D-Day.

The Queen and Prince Philip would also visit a Commonwealth War Graves cemetery in nearby Bayeux. This location contained the buried bodies of 4,144 soldiers – 338 of them have never been identified.

The Queen spoke at a state banquet in Paris that evening, being held in her honour. Reflecting on the day's proceedings, Elizabeth II spoke about her pride at the courage of those soldiers, many of whom had died so that France, and Europe, would be free.

She added, "With sorrow and regret, remembering the loss of so many fine young soldiers, sailors and airmen; with pride, at the sheer courage of the men who stormed those beaches, embodied in the veterans among us; and with thankfulness, knowing that today our nations are free and sovereign because allied forces liberated this continent from occupation and tyranny.

"Knitted together by common experiences of struggle, sacrifice and reconciliation, we remember those times in a way that strengthens unity and understanding between us".

On the final day of her visit, the Queen returned to the centre of Paris where a flower market had been renamed in her honour. It was located near Notre Dame Cathedral, and would now be known as Marche aux Fleurs-Reine Elizabeth II.

The gesture did not receive universal support among the Parisians. Some left wing city counsellors had grumbled that it was ridiculous for an unelected monarch to receive such an accolade in a country famous for having rid itself of the monarchy some 200 years earlier. They were a minority however. Most of the French people held the Queen in great respect.

The crowds in Paris that morning were especially large, with many people thrilled to catch a glimpse of the British monarch.

A young woman named Marie told reporters, "It's probably the last time we'll get to see her in France. I think it's important to see her once in your life. She's the last great monarch of Europe. I love the fact that she's England personified. Here in France, we elect presidents that come and go every five years, but the Queen remains the symbol of her country no matter where she goes".

Motorcycle policemen escort the car carrying Britain's Queen Elizabeth II and French President Francois Hollande as it drives down the Champs-Elysees avenue, June 5, 2014

THE QUEEN VISITS NORTHERN IRELAND

Queen Elizabeth II meets Northern Ireland First Minister Peter Robinson (centre) and Deputy First Minister, Martin McGuinness (R)

The Queen visited Northern Ireland in July 2014. It was the first time she had been to the country since part of her Diamond Jubilee celebrations two years earlier.

To begin the three day visit, the Queen and Duke of Edinburgh arrived at Hillsborough Castle, her official residence in Northern Ireland.

There she held separate private meetings with Northern Ireland's first and deputy first ministers, Peter Robinson and Martin McGuiness.

McGuiness, a former IRA leader turned Sinn Fein politician, spoke of how her visit was "about reaching out the hand of friendship to the unionist community".

"Reconciliation requires bold gestures and this is the third time that I had meet Queen Elizabeth as part of that continuing process."

Robinson, the Democratic Ulster Party, leader, also spoke of his adoration for Her Majesty when he said,

"I think the fact the deputy first minister is sitting with an audience with the Queen at this moment perhaps demonstrates just how far we have come".

As this was happening, Prince Philip met and spoke with around 75 people who had received the Duke of Edinburgh gold awards.

To put it simply, her second day in Northern Ireland was a big moment for pop-culture.

The Queen travelled to Belfast's Titanic Quarter, which is named for the famous ship that was constructed there. She also went to the Paint Hall Studios, where much of the hit HBO TV show *Game of Thrones* is filmed.

The television series has been a massive boon for Northern Ireland's entertainment industry, as well as its tourism industry as eager fans travel to the country eager to recognise sites from the fictional land of Westeros.

The show is estimated to have contributed around £82 million to the Northern Ireland economy, as well as 900 full-time and 5,700 part-time jobs.

The Queen wouldn't comment on whether she is a *Game of Thrones* fan, but her youngest son Prince Edward and his wife Sophie are believed to be avid viewers.

The Queen met the show creators David Benioff and Dan Weiss, as well as key members of the cast, including Kit Harrington (who plays Jon Snow), Lena Headey (Cersei Lannister), Maise Williams (Ayra Stark), Sophie Turner (Sansa Stark), and Rose Leslie (Ygritte).

Lena Headey would later admit to feeling very nervous as she was formally introduced. "I didn't think I was and then I saw her appear and I sudden thought, 'it's the Queen, the real Queen'! She was really cool, gorgeous and delightful.

"I think of everything she had done and everything she has achieved and the fact she is still interested even though she has met countless people and talked about numerous things."

According to Kit Harrington, "Being here and meeting the Queen, it's pretty amazing that the show has done that and she has come to see the sets. It gives it some sense of scale. She is an incredible person. She has an incredible presence about her. To meet someone who has been on the throne as long as she has and has seen the things she has, it's quite an experience".

Production staff gave her a short overview of the series, as well as the impact it has had on Northern Ireland.

They viewed some of the props featured on the TV show. What both show-enthusiasts and photographers wanted the most though was for the Queen to take a seat on the 'Iron Throne'. It would probably have been the only time an actual King or Queen sat on the famous chair. Instead, they had to make do with photos of Her Majesty standing next to the prop in a pale yellow dress and hat, with a slightly bemused expression on her face.

Kit Harrington would later tell British talk show host Graham Norton that he and fellow cast members did try to convince the Queen to sit on the chair, but were told in no uncertain terms by her minders that she was not allowed to sit on thrones other than her own, fictional or otherwise.

Maise Williams later said, "she (the Queen) kept commenting on how uncomfortable the throne looked, that was funny".

As she left, the production crew gave her a gift – a miniature Iron Throne replica.

On the final day of her visit, the Queen popped in for a visit to the set of another TV series. The BBC's *Antiques Roadshow* is extremely popular in England. It showcases the private collections of people, ranging from ordinary citizens to the rich and famous. The Queen visited them as they filmed in the Hillsborough Castle grounds.

From there, the Queen travelled to Coleraine. Despite soft rain falling, a healthy crowd waved union flags and welcomed Her Majesty to the township.

Local resident Elizabeth McMullan told the *Irish Times*, "We came here to celebrate the visit of the Queen. It was very pleasant, very joyful and certainly a lovely send-off for her as well".

At the end of 2014, as part of her traditional Christmas speech broadcast to the United Kingdom, the Queen recalled her visit to Northern Ireland.

"The benefits of reconciliation were clear to see when I visited Belfast in June. While my tour of the set of Game of Thrones may have gained the most attention, my visit to the Crumlin Road Gaol will remain vividly in my mind.

"What was once a prison during the Troubles is now a place of hope and fresh purpose, a reminder of what is possible when people reach out to one another, rather like the couple in the sculpture."

THE PRESIDENT OF SINGAPORE VISITS

The President of Singapore, Dr Tony Tan Keng Yam, paid a state visit to the United Kingdom in October 2014. He was accompanied by his wife, Mary Chee Bee Kiang.

For the entirety of their visit, the pair stayed at Buckingham Palace as official guests of Queen Elizabeth II and the Duke of Edinburgh.

Their state visit started on 20 October 2014. Their plane arrived privately at Heathrow Airport where they were greeted by The Viscount Hood, Lord-in-Waiting, on behalf of The Queen.

The following day, President Tan was greeted by both the Duke and Duchess of Cambridge, again on behalf of the Queen. Prince William and Catherine then accompanied the President and his wife to Horse Guards Parade. The Queen and Duke of Edinburgh officially received them there with a formal welcome.

There were presentations and a Royal Salute, while the Singapore National Anthem played.

The President, his wife, the Queen and the Duke of Edinburgh then travelled the distance along The Mall back to Buckingham Palace on board a state carriage.

The Queen and Dr Tan rode aboard the biggest carriage of them all, the Diamond Jubilee State Coach. It had only just been brought into usage, with its first run being in June when the British Parliament opened.

Next in the procession was the Australian State Coach carrying Prince Philip and Mrs Mary Tan, while behind that was the Scottish State Coach with the Duke and Duchess of Cambridge and ministers of the Singapore government.

They enjoyed a private lunch at Buckingham Palace, and afterwards The Queen invited President Tan and his wife to take a look at an exhibition of

Singapore-related items from the Royal Collection in the picture gallery.

Later in the afternoon, President Tan travelled to Westminster Abbey, where he laid a wreath at the Tomb of the Unknown Warrior and met with the Speaker of the House of Commons.

That evening, came the big State Banquet dinner hosted by the Queen. Among the attendees were Prime Minister David Cameron and his wife Samantha, Foreign Secretary Philip Hammond, Chancellor George Osborne, the Duke of York and the Earl and Countess of Wessex.

Around 170 guests gathered at the Buckingham Palace ballroom and enjoyed stuffed pheasant, salad and iced chocolate.

The Queen wore a cream-coloured gown, Queen Mary's Girls of Great Britain and Ireland tiara, and the Queen Victoria necklace. She also wore a red and white Order of Temasek sash and white star. President Tan wore his Grand Cross of the Order of Bath.

The ballroom had been decorated with elaborate floral displays, featuring autumnal reds, oranges and yellows – as well as, in tribute to Singapore and its national flower, the orchid.

During the dinner, the Queen gave a speech, again welcoming the President to the country and highlighting the close links between the United Kingdom and Singapore.

"Looking back at half a century of co-operation and ahead to new chapters in our story, it is clear that our countries remain firm friends.

"I have no doubt that by maintaining long-standing commitments to openness, fairness and enterprise, this friendship will not only be sustained but will flourish and thrive."

For his part, Dr Tan paid tribute to the royal family and for the United Kingdom's hospitality. "The people of Singapore have genuine affection for Your Majesty", he said.

And speaking of that 2012 visit by the Duke and Duchess of Cambridge, the President noted that it "further endeared the royal family to a younger generation of Singaporeans".

She also thanked the President for having given a warm welcome to her grandson William and his wife during their trip to Singapore in 2012 as part of the Diamond Jubilee celebrations.

The next day, the Duke of York, Prince Andrew, accompanied the President and his wife on a visit to the Royal Society. President Tan received the Royal Society King Charles II Medal, as recognition for his support in science and innovation.

That evening, President Tan met with United Kingdom Prime Minister David Cameron.

The Singapore President's visit continued on 23 October with the Queen and Duke of Edinburgh formally bidding farewell to their guests at Buckingham Palace. This was not the end of the state visit for the President however. He would spend two more days in the country, travelling and meeting various people before returning home to Singapore.

Main pic (opposite page): Queen Elizabeth II greets the President of Singapore Tony Tan Keng Yam during a ceremonial welcome at Horse Guards Parade, October 21, 2014

Above: Singapore's President Tony Tan Keng Yam (RC) stands to address a banquet in his honour at the Guildhall, October 22, 2014

GALLIPOLI ANNIVERSARY

The 100th anniversary of the 'Gallipoli Campaign' took place in April 2015. This was a campaign that took place during the First World War, between 25 April 1915 and 9 January 1916.

The Gallipoli Peninsula is Turkish-land on the northern bank of the Dardenelles, a strait that offers a sea route to Russia. In a bid to capture it, the Allied Powers launched a naval attack and amphibious landing on the peninsula. The ultimate aim, after taking the peninsula, would be to advance to Constantinople, the capital of the then Ottoman Empire, and thus force their surrender.

It was an unmitigated disaster. The initial landings did not go as well as the Allies had hoped and both sides soon became stuck in the same trench warfare that was seen right across the First World War battlefields. Eventually the Allies pulled out, but not before great loss of life on both sides.

In total, 131,000 troops would die at Gallipoli. On the Allied side, there were 25,000 British military personnel who lost their life, as well as 10,000 from Australia and New Zealand.

Even as the war brought about the ultimate undoing of the Ottoman Empire, the defence of Gallipoli solidified Turkish pride and nationalism.

For the Allies, it was an utter humiliation. Winston Churchill, then First Lord of the Admiralty, suffered a huge blow to his reputation in Great Britain and would take years to recover.

It also marked somewhat of a birth of national consciousness for both Australia and New Zealand. Originally British colonies, the two countries had become 'dominions' within the British Empire, within the past couple of decades. At the outset of war, they were still closely linked to their parent country. Members of the Australian and New Zealand Army Corps (referred to as ANZACs) were among the largest casualties during the Gallipoli campaign. Anger back home at the huge loss of life, and at what British command had led them into, started a process of both Australians and New Zealanders gradually moving away from the influence of the United Kingdom.

The date, 25 April would later become a National Holiday in both Australia and New Zealand, called 'ANZAC Day'. It commemorated the war service of all soldiers, but the history of the Gallipoli campaign is of special significance to this day.

And so, 100 years after that infamous campaign got underway, the Royal Family helped mark the commemorations at home in the United Kingdom, as well as abroad.

Queen Elizabeth II laid a wreath at the Cenotaph in Whitehall. She was joined by the Duke of Edinburgh, Prince William, United Kingdom Prime Minister David Cameron as well as politicians for the memorial parade.

Prince Philip, Duke of Edinburgh, Prince William Duke of Cambridge and Queen Elizabeth II attend the wreath-laying ceremony at the Cenotaph to commemorate ANZAC Day and the Centenary of the Gallipoli Campaign, April 25, 2015

Prime Minister Cameron would also lay his own wreath, as did Australia's Attorney-General George Brandis and New Zealand Speaker of the House of Representatives David Carter.

As the clock struck 11am, there were two minutes of silence, before Big Ben tolled.

A special moment came during the reading of the famous Laurence Binyon poem For the Fallen. It contains the line "They shall not grow old, as we that are left grow old", which is repeated at Remembrance Day and ANZAC Day ceremonies across the Commonwealth. For this particular service, it was read by 22 year old Michael Toohey. His great uncle, Private Thomas Toohey, served in the Royal Dublin Fishers, and was killed in action during a Gallipoli landing at V Beach in Cape Helles on 25 April 1915. Private Thomas Toohey was also just 22 years old.

Her Majesty then joined a service of remembrance at Westminster Abbey, where she laid a wreath at the Grave of the Unknown Warrior.

The national flags of the United Kingdom, Australia, New Zealand and Turkey were all carried through Westminster Abbey and placed close to the high altar. The inclusion of the Turkish flag was significant as it marked a sign of reconciliation between old enemies.

The Very Reverend Doctor John Hall, Dean of Westminster, told the congregation, "We honour today the courage of the men at Gallipoli. The memory of the Great War provides for us warning and encouragement. We are warned that war must involve terrible suffering and death. We are encouraged by the spirit of national pride and determination by those we remember this ANZAC Day."

Meanwhile, Prince Charles and Prince Harry travelled to the Gallipoli peninsula in Turkey to attend services there.

On the evening before ANZAC Day, they visited the Helles Memorial. This memorial on the southern tip of the peninsula serves as a Commonwealth battle memorial for the entire Gallipoli campaign, as well as a place of commemoration for all those who died and have no known grave. Prince Charles read an extract from Gallipoli by John Masefield, and Prince Harry read an extract from The Bathe by AP Herbert.

The following morning at dawn, both Prince Charles and Prince Harry joined other world leaders, including Australian Prime Minister Tony Abbott and New Zealand Prime Minister John Key, at Anzac Cove. Prince Charles laid a wreath, and in his speech, focussed on the words a soldier had written to his wife on the eve of battle. The soldier had told her how much he loved and her and his kids, and wished he could come home and see them again. But he understood his duty to fight, come what may.

Prince Charles, Prince of Wales and Australian Major General Mark Kelly attend a ceremony marking the 100th anniversary of the Battle of Gallipoli, at Anzac Cove in Gallipoli, Turkey, April 25, 2015

THE BIRTH OF PRINCESS CHARLOTTE

On 8 September 2014, Clarence House announced that Catherine, the Duchess of Cambridge, was expecting her second child.

On 2 May 2015, at approximately 8.34am, the Duchess gave birth to a daughter at St Mary's Hospital in London. She weighed 8lbs 3oz (3.71kg). In contrast to the first labour, this baby was born in two-and-a-half hours.

The announcement came first on social media. The Duke and Duchess of Cambridge using Twitter to let the world know a girl had been born. It came from the Kensington Palace Twitter account (@KensingtonRoyal), "Her Royal Highness, the Duchess of Cambridge was safely delivered of a daughter at 8.34am".

The baby was delivered naturally by midwives Arona Ahmed and Jacquie Dunkley-Bent. Other doctors present included Alan Farthing, surgeon-gynaecologist to Queen Elizabeth II, Guy Thorpe-Beeston, an expert in high risk pregnancies and surgeon-gynaecologist of the Royal Household, Sunit Godambe, consultant neonatologist at the hospital, and Huw Thomas, physician to the Queen.

Just ten hours after the girl was born, she was shown off to the adoring crowd outside the hospital. Proud parents Catherine and William holding her and smiling.

On the evening of the following day, London showed just how it felt about the arrival of a new Princess. Well-known landmarks such as the Tower Bridge, the London Eye and Trafalgar Square fountains were illuminated in pink to mark the birth.

On Monday 4 May, gun salutes were fired at Hyde Park. Soldiers from The King's Troop Royal Horse Artillery rode out in a procession from Wellington Barracks to sound out 41 shots from cannons.

At the same time, the Honourable Artillery Company departed their Armoury House barracks within the City of London to fire a 62-gun salute from the Tower of London.

The world also found out the girl's name later that day. Over the days since her birth, there had been all sorts of betting activity on what the name might be. Alice and Charlotte were the two favourites, but the betting markets were also mindful that the Duke and Duchess may want to be a bit sentimental and name the child either Elizabeth or Diana.

Clarence House revealed she would be known as Princess Charlotte Elizabeth Diana. That they chose Charlotte as her first name was likely in honour of her grandfather Prince

Prince William, Duke of Cambridge and Catherine, Duchess of Cambridge depart the Lindo Wing with their new baby daughter at St Mary's Hospital, May 2, 2015

Main pic: Catherine, Duchess of Cambridge, Prince William, Duke of Cambridge, Princess Charlotte of Cambridge and Prince George of Cambridge talk to Queen Elizabeth II, Prince Phillip, Duke of Cambridge and Camilla, Duchess of Cornwall at the Church of St Mary Magdalene after the Christening of Princess Charlotte of Cambridge, July 5, 2015

Inset: Prince William, Duke of Cambridge, Prince George of Cambridge, Catherine Duchess of Cambridge and Princess Charlotte of Cambridge arrive at the Church of St Magdalene, July 5, 2015

Charles. And indeed, both middle names were also very significant. Elizabeth was for her great grandmother, Queen Elizabeth II. And Diana was for the grandmother she would never get to meet, Princess Diana.

The name was made official a day later when Kensington Palace tweeted a picture of her official birth certificate, filed by Prince William. He listed his occupation as, simply, Prince of the United Kingdom.

That same day, Queen Elizabeth II was able to meet her newest grandchild for the first time at Kensington Palace. She had been staying at her Sandringham estate in Norfolk when the baby was born and had arrived in London that day. She spent 20 minutes with the Duke and Duchess of Cambridge, as well as young Charlotte.

The meeting marked the first time in 118 years a serving sovereign had met a great-granddaughter born in direct succession on the male line. This hadn't happened since Queen Victoria met George VI's sister Princess Mary in 1897.

Prince Harry, who was in Australia when Princess Charlotte was born, also told reporters his niece looked "absolutely beautiful". He would also later admit, while touring New Zealand, that the arrival of another baby for his older brother had got him thinking about his own plans for children. Although, since he was single, he added "There come times when you think now is the time to settle down, or now is not, whatever way it is, but I don't think you can force these things, it will happen when it's going to happen".

On 7 June, Kensington Palace released the first official photos of Princess Charlotte, alongside her older brother Prince George. He was almost 2 years old, and was pictured smiling as he held his younger sister. One especially cute picture showed little George leaning in to kiss his sister on her forehead.

On 5 July 2015, Princess Charlotte was christened by the Archbishop of Canterbury at St Mary Magdalene Church in Sandringham. Her godparents were The Hon. Laura Fellowes, Prince William's maternal cousin; Adam Middleton, the Duchess's paternal cousin, and family friends Thomas van Straubenzee, James Meade and Sophie Carter.

A Kensington Palace spokesman described the day as magical. "The Duke and Duchess of Cambridge and their whole family had a wonderful day on Sunday and were delighted to share the special occasion with the thousands of people who came to Sandringham"

More official photographs were released to the public, including one image of William holding Prince George and Catherine holding Princess Charlotte in the gardens of Sandringham House.

Another image showed members of the royal family and the Middleton family together for a family portrait inside Sandringham House. The Queen, dressed in a floral white dress with a pink coat and hat, sat seated on a lounge chair, alongside Prince William, Prince George, Catherine and Princess Charlotte.

VE DAY 60TH ANNIVERSARY CELEBRATIONS

The middle of 2015 marked 70 years since the Allied Powers claimed 'Victory in Europe', by defeating Nazi Germany in the Second World War.

The three-day long series of commemorations began at 3pm on Friday 8 May, the approximate time Sir Winston Churchill began his broadcast to the United Kingdom, declaring the Second World War to be over. There was a Service of Remembrance at the Cenotaph.

That evening, the Queen lit the first of 200 beacons that would light up the night sky. Accompanied by the Duke of Edinburgh, the Queen lit the beacon at Windsor Great Park at approximately 9.30pm to mark the moment peace was declared some 70 years earlier. Two minutes later, beacons were lit and burned right across the United Kingdom.

At 11am on Saturday 9 May, the bells of cathedrals and churches across the country rang out in a sign of victory. It symbolised the end to the years the bells had remained silent during the war years.

Among the churches involved were St Paul's Cathedral in London, as well as Westminster Abbey. While the HMS Ocean, one of the Royal Navy's largest ships, sounded its horn.

The celebrations then continued into the evening with a concert at Horse Guards Parade in London. Some of the artists to perform included veteran rockers Status Quo, opera diva Katherina Jenkins, and pop singer Pixie Lott. Spectators waved flags as the artists performed a mix of their own music, as well as 1940s-inpired songs.

On Sunday 10 May, Queen Elizabeth II joined a Service of Thanksgiving at Westminster Abbey.

She was present as a wreath was laid at the Tomb of the Unknown Warrior.

Among the audience were Prince Charles and Camilla the Duchess of Cornwall, as well as several other members of the royal family, and thousands of veterans. Also in attendance were representatives of the Allied and Commonwealth nations that fought alongside the United Kingdom.

Archbishop of Canterbury Justin Welby addressed the service, "We gather again, 70 years on, thankful for victory over the greatest darkness of the 20th century, perhaps of all history".

"The peace for which we give thanks today... remains an ongoing project of reconciliation, not only for us but as a gift to the world, where conflict and extremism destroy hope, devastate prosperity, vanquish aspiration to a better life."

Actor Simon Russell Beale read a passage from the VE Day speech delivered by the Queen's father King George VI.

Sir Winston Churchill's great-granddaughter Zoe Churchill read the act of rededication along with VE Day veteran John Wilson.

After the service had concluded, the Queen was introduced to veterans of the Second World War.

Later in the day, thousands lined the streets in central London to watch an Armed Forces and Veteran's Parade to Buckingham Palace.

A fly-past of World War Two aircraft was conducted, including a display by the Red Arrows, the Royal Air Force's acrobatic team. Prince Charles and the Duchess of Cornwall viewed this from Horse Guards Parade, where Prince Charles also took the salute.

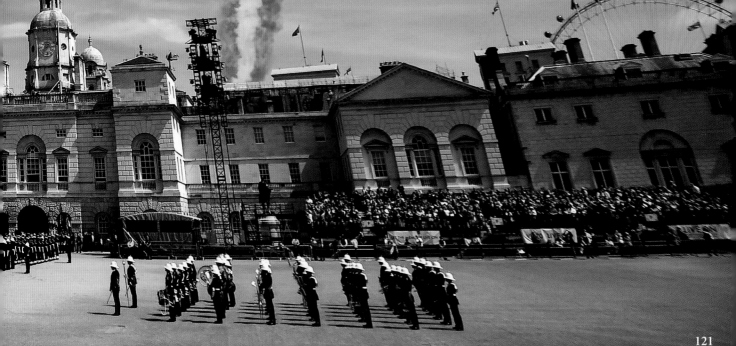

TROOPING THE COLOUR

The 89th birthday celebrations for Queen Elizabeth II continued with the traditional Trooping the Colour ceremony.

Trooping the Colour is a ceremony performed by regiments of the British and Commonwealth armies, dating back to the 17th century.

It's also a special occasion for the British sovereign as it marks their official birthday.

It's traditionally held on a Saturday in June on Horse Guards Parade in St James Park.

The occasion also features 'The Queen's Birthday Parade' broadcast live on the BBC and internationally. The Queen travels down The Mall from Buckingham Palace in a royal procession, escorted by the Household Cavalry.

Once at Horse Guards Parade, the Queen receives a royal salute, inspects her troops of the Household

Division and the Kings Troop. Each year, one of the foot-guards regiments is selected to troop its colour through the ranks of guards. Then the entire Household Division assembly conducted a march past the Queen, who receives a salute from the salute base.

Music is provided by the massed bands of foot guards, as well as a Corps of Drums.

The Queen then returns to Buckingham Palace and watches another march.

A 41-gun salute is sounded by the King's Troop in Green Park, and then the Queen and other members of the Royal Family appear before the public on the Buckingham Palace balcony for a Royal Air Force flypast.

Queen Elizabeth has attended almost every Trooping the Colour ceremony since ascending the throne. The only exception being in 1955 when a national rail strike called the whole thing off.

For the 2015 edition, the monarch inspected 1,100 soldiers of the Household Division at Horse Guards Parade in central London.

Accompanied by the Duke of Edinburgh, the Queen arrived in an Ascot Landau vintage carriage after the short drive down The Mall from Buckingham Palace.

She wore a peach and silver dress and coat as well as a matching hat. The previous time she had worn this ensemble was for the Diamond Jubilee horse pageant in May 2012.

The royal family would later appear on the balcony at Buckingham Palace. They watched 31 aircraft – including Spitfires and Hurricanes – soar overhead.

This balcony appearance also marked the first time the Duchess of Cambridge had made an appearance since the birth of Princess Charlotte, six weeks earlier. The crowds below were thrilled to catch a glimpse of not only Princess Catherine, but also of the baby girl in her mother's arms.

LONDON, ENGLAND - JUNE 13: (L-R) Princess Anne, Princess Royal, Camilla, Duchess of Cornwall, Prince Charles, Prince of Wales, Prince George of Cambridge,Prince William, Duke of Cambridge, Catherine, Duchess of Cambridge, Queen Elizabeth II, James, Viscount Severn, Prince Harry, Prince Philip, Duke of Edinburgh and Prince Andrew, Duke of York look out on the balcony of Buckingham Palace during the Trooping the Colour, June 13, 2015

A VISIT TO GERMANY

Queen Elizabeth II and German President Joachim Gauck meet pupils outside Schloss Bellevue Palace in Berlin, Germany, June 24, 2015

Germany welcomed Queen Elizabeth II with a 21 gun salute and the roar of Luftwaffe Fighter Jets overhead.

The Queen and Prince Philip had arrived in the country on 23 June 2015 via a chartered plane. They landed at Berlin Tegel airport, accompanied by two Eurofighter Typhoon jets.

The royal couple were in Germany on invitation from the country's President Joachim Guack. It was the seventh time the Queen has visited Germany, and the fifth as an official state visit. Her first visit as Queen came in 1965, and the most recent had been in 2004.

Cheering crowds greeted the Queen and Prince Philip in Berlin.

As they arrived at Tegel Airport, artillery gunners fired a 21-gun salute, and fighter jets flew overhead in ceremonial formation.

German newspapers had eagerly awaited this royal arrival. The tabloid *Bild* had run a supplement in its Tuesday print edition containing a poster of the Queen in a bright pink outfit and matching hat alongside the caption "Herzlich Wilkommen Ma'am" (Warm Welcome Ma'am).

They started the day at Berlin's Bellevue Palace where they were greeted by President Gauck and his partner Daniela Schadt.

The Queen strolled across the palace grounds alongside the President, for a formal greeting by a military honour guard. A band played 'God Save The Queen' as well as the German national anthem.

They then went for a boat ride along the Spree River. The Queen waved to hundreds of school children who had packed bridges along the route, waving German and British flags.

The Queen also spent some time meeting Germany's chancellor Angela Merkel. This visit was seen as being potentially important in the German government's effort to convince the United Kingdom to remain a part of the European Union. The UK is due to hold a referendum in 2017 on the issue, and Prime Minister David Cameron was set to meet European Union leaders in Brussels.

The Queen would explore the issue publicly during the state banquet, held at Bellevue Palace.

"In our lives, Mr President, we have seen the worst but also the best of our continent. We have witnessed how quickly things can change for the better. But we know that we must work hard to maintain the benefits of the post-war world.

"We know that division in Europe is dangerous and that we must guard against it in the West as well as in the East of our continent. That remains a common endeavour."

An important part of the Queen's visit came on the final day when she went to the Bergen-Belsen concentration camp.

This was the site of many atrocities during the Second World War. As many as 70,000 people – 30,000 of them Jewish, and 20,000 Soviets – are believed to have died here.

This marked the first time a British monarch had visited a concentration camp. Bergen-Belsen was the only such camp that had been liberated by British forces during the Second World War. This happened on 13 April 1945.

As their visit got underway, the Queen and Prince Philip were welcomed by the director of the Bergen-Belsen memorial, Christian Wagner. He pointed them towards a simple gravestone in memory of Anne Frank, the teenage girl whose diary would become a post-war bestseller. She and her sister Margot had died at Bergen-Belsen in 1945. Like many gravestones there, this is not the actual last resting place of Anne Frank's remains.

Dressed in a grey cashmere coat and hat, The Queen laid a wreath for the dead at the Inscription Wall and obelisk. This memorial honours every victim from every country.

She also met with a group of concentration camp survivors and liberators, as well as representatives from religious communities.

In speaking with survivors, the Queen and Prince Philip sought to understand the horrific conditions these people had endured.

"It was more like dying, not living" told Anita Lasker-Wallfisch, a German Jew. "Belsen was complete chaos. People were sent there and sat there and waited until they were dead. When the British came it was a miracle, we thought we were dreaming, suddenly we heard an English voice."

One of the voices was liberator Captain Eric Brown, who recounted his memories to the Queen. "This was just a field of corpses."

To which the Queen responded, "It must have been horrific really".

Brown later told reporters the Queen was extremely respectful, "She was listening very carefully. I would say she was quite affected by the atmosphere here. You can't avoid it, can you".

The Queen and Prince Philip were given the opportunity to spend some time alone, to contemplate the atrocities of this place in private, away from the photographers and minders.

They took a half-hour walk around the camp on their own. There was quiet as they passed by graves, the only sounds being the birds in the distance. Then they walked alone into the House of Silence, a building where visitors can sit under a glass roof and reflect.

Queen Elizabeth II and Prince Philip, Duke of Edinburgh lay a wreath at the inscription wall during their visit of the concentration camp memorial at Bergen-Belsen in Lohheide, Germany, June 26, 2015

90TH BIRTHDAY CELEBRATIONS

On 21 April 2016, Her Majesty Queen Elizabeth II will turn 90 years old. She is already the longest-lived British monarch. Queen Victoria died at the age of 81, as did King George II as the oldest male ruler. This all means that never before will the United Kingdom have celebrated the 90th birthday of their sovereign.

The Queen's actual birthday on 21 April is expected to be celebrated as a mostly private affair. This is what the Queen prefers to do, leaving the more extravagant public celebrations for the summer. Those celebrations are expected to be as big a birthday party the United Kingdom has ever seen.

At the time of writing, organisers are planning three days of events over the traditional June period when the Queen's Birthday is officially celebrated. This will be from Friday 10 June through to Sunday 12 June 2016.

Beginning on the Friday, the Queen and Prince Philip (who will turn 95 on this day) are scheduled to attend a thanksgiving service at St Paul's Cathedral.

The following day, the Queen and other members of the royal family will watch a special Trooping the Colour at Horse Guard's Parade.

And to round out the celebrations there will be the largest ever street-party held in Britain.

More than ten thousand people will be able to visit The Mall on Sunday 12 June. Guests, including those from the hundreds of charities supported by the Queen, will be invited for a hamper-style lunch. Members of the public will also get invitations, to be handed out via special public ballot system.

Alongside the Queen, other royal attendees are expected to include Prince Philip and grandsons Prince William and Prince Harry.

This event is expected to raise money for a newly-created Patron's Charity that supports the Queen's various causes. The Queen is patron of organisations such as the British Diabetic Association, the Scouts Association and the Great Ormond Street Hospital.

Tables will be decorated with flags lining the kilometre long route from Buckingham Palace.

For those unable to get a ticket, giant screens will be erected in both Green Park and St James Park televising the day's events, including various entertainers performing.

The Queen's grandson Peter Phillips is director of a global events agency, and has come up with the idea for this particular event. It's expected The Mall street party will coincide with thousands of other street parties held right across the United Kingdom that day.

"We are aiming to inspire as many people as we can to host street parties of their own for the direct benefit of their community. I hope that people in Britain and across the Commonwealth dust off their picnic tables and join us in celebration this very special occasion."

Guests listen during a speech by Britain's Queen Elizabeth II in honour of the President of Ireland Michael D. Higgins at the State Banquet during the Irish president's state visit in Windsor, west of London, April 8, 2014